Casa California

SPANISH-STYLE HOUSES FROM SANTA BARBARA TO SAN CLEMENTE

TEXT BY ELIZABETH MCMILLIAN | PHOTOGRAPHS BY MELBA LEVICK

FOREWORD BY DAVID GEBHARD

Casa California

SPANISH-STYLE HOUSES FROM SANTA BARBARA TO SAN CLEMENTE

First published in the United States of America in 1996 by
Rizzoli International Publications, Inc.
300 Park Avenue South, New York NY 10010

Library of Congress Cataloging-in-Publication Data

McMillian, Elizabeth Jean.
Casa California : Spanish-style houses from Santa Barbara to San Clemente
Text by Elizabeth McMillian ; photographs by Melba Levick ;
foreword by David Gebhard.
p. cm.
ISBN 0-8478-1850-0 (hc)
1. Architecture, Domestic—California, Southern. 2. Architecture, Spanish—Influence. 3. Regionalism in architecture—California, Southern.
I. Levick, Melba. II. Title.
NA7235.C22.S686 1996
728'.37'097949—dc20 95-45722
CIP

Designed by Sisco & Evans, New York

Black and white photographs pp. 14–19 by Elizabeth McMillian

Front jacket illustration: Battistone House, Hope Ranch, Santa Barbara
Back jacket illustration: Breakfast room, Casa de las Campanas, Hancock Park
Frontispiece: Casa de las Campanas, Hancock Park
p. 6: Wrought iron lamp detail, Casa del Herrero, Montecito
p. 12: Chandelier and clerestory window, Casa Pacifica, San Clemente
pp. 20–21: The Andalusia Courtyard Apartments, Hollywood

Reprinted in 1997, 1999

Printed and bound in Singapore

Contents

Foreword

DAVID GEBHARD

In a 1926 article, "The Mediterranean Influence," the architecture journalist-critic Henry H. Saylor laid down two cardinal principles that he felt underlay all architectural design. "We must," he wrote, "perforce build in a so-called architectural style; there is no way of speaking architecturally excepting in one of its understood tongues.

"Nevertheless," he went on, "if we would produce architecture and not archaeology we must adapt rather than copy." He further stated, "What we mean by architectural adaptation is the absorption of the spirit of an architectural language and the re-phrasing of it in the vernacular of today." [1] The view that one must add to traditional languages, not simply copy them, was the guiding principle in the 1910s and 1920s for all of the period styles then in vogue, including those referred to as Mediterranean, Italian, or Spanish.

The mid- to late twenties marked a high point in the popularity of Mediterranean-Hispanic-inspired architecture throughout America, especially for suburban houses. The enthusiasm for these architectural images is easy to understand when one observes the self-conscious regionalism cultivated in those portions of the country that had formerly belonged to Spain or Mexico: Florida, Texas and the Southwest, and, of course, California.

Europe's obsession with nationalism and symbols of nationalism was certainly one of the believed-in fictions that encouraged California's mission revival (ca. 1890–1920) and other, similarly self-conscious regional Hispanic architecture in Texas, the American Southwest, and Florida.[2] As was the case with the nationalist architecture of Europe, America's West Coast mission revival would not come about until the Europeans discovered that vernacular folk architecture must form the core of any readable regional or national style.

However, the regional basis for Hispanic architecture does not explain why this imagery came to be so broadly accepted throughout the country. Perhaps the answer in part is to be found in the contemporary view that Spain expressed more of a sense of romance and fantasy than did any other European country. In the 1920s, allusions to the romantic spirit in architecture consisted of two ingredients: the aura of the exotic and faraway, and a feeling that the past could be played against the present.

"There are two reasons for the strongly individual character of the Spanish arts," wrote Robert L. Ames in 1923:

> First, they have been powerfully influenced by the Moorish civilization which persisted for centuries after Moorish rule in Spain was finally destroyed [the exotic and faraway], and second, due to the fact that Spain is geographically almost cut off from contact with the rest of Europe, occupying a peninsula

> which is shut in by the rocky Pyrenees, Spain has been passed by the march of progress and has remaine undisturbed. . . . Excepting in a few large cities, Spain is very nearly as medieval as when Columbus visited the court of Ferdinand and Isabella, and Spanish art retains much of its primitive simplicity [the past played against the present].[3]

If one looks at illustrations in children's books published from 1900 through the 1930s, one frequently encounters images of medieval towns, cottages, and castles. When the stories demanded more exotic settings, the images, more often than not, were Islamic. Although usually not geographically specific, many of the images of imaginary castles set upon precipitous rocky hills, and of villages composed of white-walled and tile-roofed houses in hilly open landscapes, came close to matching what one could actually see in Spain from the turn of the century through the 1930s.[4]

Contemporaneous with the interest in Spain's architecture was a developing enthusiasm for Mexico. Articles on and illustrations of Mexican architecture were published in American magazines and architecture journals from the 1880s through the 1930s.[5] In early 1892, the young architect Bertram G. Goodhue made the first of a series of trips to Mexico. He published his initial experience along with sketches in a playful and charming little volume, *Mexican Memories*. His enthusiastic reaction to the country is apparent in many passages. "Fancy," he wrote, "a landscape in which long reaches of uncultivated fields and masses of graceful foliage contend for the mastery, and dotted here and there with patches of white, which as you approach . . . resolve themselves into small Indian towns, white-walled and low, in the midst of which rise . . . tiled dome and rococo towers. . . ."[6] Goodhue's Mexican experience, coupled with his memories of Spain and Italy, formed the basis for the idealized Hispanic city he later created in Balboa Park in San Diego for the 1915 Panama-California International Exposition.

It was often argued then and still is now by advocates of modernism that sentimental romanticism of this sort was nothing more than a deplorable form of escapism on the part of the American middle and upper-middle classes. In opposition to this view, the defenders of traditionalism continually pointed out that this particular brand of romanticism should not be looked upon as a form of escapism but rather as an indication of the triumph of the child over the adult. Especially in the teens and twenties, many adults felt that they no longer had to put on the "false" guise of adulthood; they could see and experience the world with the purity and delight of a child.

In a none too approving fashion, Lewis Mumford wrote in 1925:

> Our country houses and our suburban cottages are almost universally built on the principle of keeping our working and living in two different compartments. Not being able to humanize "business," we become gods when we get outside its domain; with a little architectural hocus-pocus we transport ourselves to another age, another climate, another social regime, and best of all, to another aesthetic system.[7]

The American suburban dwelling or country house and its garden provided a way to express this perception, for here the visions of childhood could be made "real" through the use of forms from the past and from exotic locales. Life in a Mediterranean-Hispanic-style or any other period revival-style house was enriched by the use of historic furniture and decorative art objects. This totalizing experience of historic garden, house, and furnishings was enriched by the "reality" that the emerging motion picture industry presented in its impressive movie sets.

If a principal goal of the architecture of the time was to establish an aura of "history, romance and poetry," there can be little doubt that the most appropriate European source was Spain and its architectural tradition.[8] The romance of Spanish buildings and gardens, as well as the response they provoked, can be sensed in a comment from an 1896 introduction to Washington Irving's tale *The Alhambra*: "[W]hen there is a story to be told, he [Irving] can be as simple and straightforward as the child's 'Once upon a time' with which he begins many a tale; appropriately, since the legends of the Alhambra are but stories for grown-up children."[9]

The way in which Spanish architecture and decorative arts entered the twentieth-century American consciousness is itself a fascinating and complex tale, an outcome of several centuries of European enchantment with Islamic architecture and decorative arts. However, by the end of the nineteenth century, Europeans also had developed an interest in their own rural and village vernacular architecture. The Europeans' fascination with Islamic architecture and decoration and with their own vernacular traditions was transferred across the Atlantic, where it was enthusiastically embraced.

Spain and Spanish imagery, then, played an intriguing role in American architecture of the late nineteenth and early twentieth centuries. From the 1850s on, Spain entered the American consciousness through the idea of the romance of the Moors. Just before and after the turn of the century, exponents of the Beaux Arts enriched this fascination with Islamic Spain by expanding their palette to include Spanish and Italian Renaissance sources. This "respectable" use of Spanish prototypes joined the remarkably popular, nationwide fascination with California's "native" mission revival style, with its stucco walls and tile roofs.

The blocks upon blocks of Spanish-style apartments, duplexes, dwellings, and bungalows built in the twenties and thirties in Los Angeles, San Diego, San Francisco, and Oakland attest to the appeal of this imagery to architects and clients throughout California. The reasons for its success were pointed out in *Spanish Homes of America,* one of the numerous popular construction pattern books issued during the 1920s: "It [the Spanish style] has the support and patronage of those of worth, and its guidance has been in the hands of a bold and daring group of artists and craftsmen. Few conventions bind it, and its plasticity—its susceptibility to varying treatment has appealed to the architect. He has refined its simplicity and developed its possibility to the point where the fame of California Spanish has reached out over the nation."[10]

The commercial success of the Spanish image, both regionally and throughout America, was in no small part due to its adaptation for the sets of numerous silent films of the twenties and to the preference for the style evident in the suburban and country houses of Hollywood stars, producers, and directors. The list of stars who lived in or commissioned Spanish revival-style houses includes most of the "greats" of those years: Charlie Chaplin, Rudolph Valentino, Douglas Fairbanks and Mary Pickford, Harold Lloyd, and Buster Keaton. Among the producers and directors were Samuel Goldwyn, Louis B. Mayer, and others. With such a populist imprint of approval, it was not surprising that Spanish revival became the latest rage in furniture, interior decoration, and architecture.

As Mary Pickford commented, "I have felt that the Spanish influence in California is one of the great charms our state possesses, a precious heritage second only to our climate, and that it should be preserved in every possible way."[11] She remarked that the reason she and her husband had selected George Washington Smith to design a Spanish-style house for them was the architect's vision as an artist. They felt that, more than anyone else, Smith could "recreate the spirit of this day [of early California], age, people and architecture."[12]

Certainly the high point of the Spanish colonial revival in California and throughout America came in the twenties, especially between the years 1924 and 1932. Spanish imagery continued to be strongly favored in California into the Depression years. Once building activity in Southern California began to recover in 1935 and 1936, Hispanic houses (now often spoken of as California ranch houses) continued to be built in large numbers. Generally the designs of the thirties tended to be somewhat abstracted and in many cases incorporated design elements associated with modern or moderne images. The most important change was the emergence of California's Monterey style and the California ranch house as the fashionable new styles. Influential and highly publicized examples of ranch houses were designed in Northern California by Clarence Tantu, Gardner Daily, and William W. Wurster; and in Southern California by Donald McMurray, H. Roy Kelley, and Roland E. Coate. As the California Monterey and ranch styles emerged in the thirties, their forms and details played an intriguing stylistc game between the intensely popular Anglo-colonial revival and the Hispanic regionalism of California.[13]

One could suggest that this surge of interest in things Hispanic was an expression of America's assumed "*Pax Romana*" protectorate over the whole of the Spanish New World. In architecture this dominance was symbolized by a sumptuous palace, the Pan American Union building in Washington, D.C., of 1910, by Paul Cret and Albert Kelsey.

The Spanish colonial revival of the later teens, and above all of the post-World War I years of the twenties, pretty well abandoned this imperialist implication. There was a general feeling that Spanish colonial revival houses, suburban dwellings, movie theaters, and retail stores represented a cultivated world of play and fun, of enjoyment and escape. Southern California, Hollywood and the silent film industry, and the well-publicized lives of the stars themselves decidedly reinforced this reaction; it was not accidental that one of the favored architectural styles for motion picture theaters of the twenties was Hispanic-Moorish.

The Depression and inward-looking nationalism of the thirties brought this Hispanic phase to an end. International sentiment, which embraced a wide variety of European period revival styles, was replaced by Anglo-American sentiment. What was left of the regional Spanish style was absorbed into the Anglo, and came to be expressed in the new vogue for the Monterey style.

A 1930 article "Els pobles espanyols de California," published in the Spanish magazine *D'Aci I D'Alla*, observed that "the American architects have found the golden mean between literal copy and the overly free interpretation. They have adapted them [Spanish images] to modern requirements without disfiguring them."[14]

Like East Coast Anglo-colonial imagery, Hispanic-Mediterranean forms incorporated a wide variety of design references—they could be sentimentally romantic to the hilt and as opulent as one might desire; or, on the other hand, simple, primitive, and vernacular, closely akin in many ways to the emerging modern imagery of the time. The style's irregular form and fenestration lent themselves easily to a wide variety of new and old building types, and the style was open to the use of new construction technologies, especially reinforced concrete. It also was compatible with one of America's least expensive means of construction, the stucco-sheathed, wood-frame building. All of these qualities were assets of the Spanish style, but in the end its wide acceptance lay, both then and now, as architect George Washington Smith observed in 1929, in its ability to express America's attachment to romance and sentiment.[15]

1. Henry H. Saylor, "The Mediterranean Influence," *Garden and Home Builder* 44 (November 1926): 207.

2. Rexford Newcomb, *Mediterranean Domestic Architecture in the United States* (Cleveland: J.H. Jansen, 1928): 1–8; David Gebhard, "Architectural Imagery, The Missions and California," *The Harvard Architectural Review* 1 (Spring 1980): 137–45.

3. Robert L. Ames, "Planning and Furnishing in the Early Spanish Style," *House Beautiful* 53 (January 1923): 16.

4. Hans Christian Andersen, the author of the widely read mid-nineteenth-century *Fairy Tales*, not only visited Spain but produced a popular guidebook to the country, *In Spain* (London: Richard Bently, 1864).

5. One of the earliest of these was a series by Sylvester Baxter, "Strolls About Mexico," Part 1, *American Architect and Building News* 14 (October 6, 1883): 159–60; Part 2, 14 (December 8, 1883): 267–68; Part 3, 35 (January 16, 1892): 43.

6. Bertram G. Goodhue, *Mexican Memories* (New York: G.M. Allen Co., 1892): 133.

7. Lewis Mumford, "The Architecture of Escape," *The New Republic* 43 (August 12, 1925): 321-22.

8. William Orr Ludlow, "Romance," *The Architectural Forum* 40 (November 1931): 559-60.

9. Elizabeth Robins Pennell, "Introduction," Washington Irving, *The Alhambra* (New York and London: Macmillan, 1896): xiii.

10. Roy A. Hilton Company, *Spanish Homes of California* (Long Beach: Roy A. Hilton Co., Publishers, 1925): 3.

11. Mary Pickford Fairbanks, "Spanish Architectural Ideals for California Home," *Architect and Engineer* 87 (December 1926): 11–12.

12. Quoted in Zoe A. Battu, "Mary Pickford—Student of Architecture," *Pacific Coast Architect* 32 (December 1927): 55.

13. David Gebhard, "The Monterey Tradition: History Reordered," *New Mexico Studies in the Fine Arts* 7 (1982): 14–19.

14. I. Abadal, "Els poples espanyols de California," *D'Aci I D'Alla* 19 (February 1930): 53–59. My translation.

15. John Taylor Boyd, Jr., "House Showing a Distinguished Simplicity" (interview with George Washington Smith), *Arts and Decoration* 33 (October 1930): 57.

Introduction

Based on California's brief period of Spanish colonization from the mid-eighteenth through the early nineteenth century, a fictional architectural heritage was produced in Southern California from the 1910s through the 1930s that gave rise to the region's most exotic, ornate, and lushly planted domestic environment. This particular Spanish revival movement was a romantic borrowing from the historical achievements of California's conquerors and had little to do with the native population's culture or ethnic heritage.

Many of the architects whose work is included in this book, such as George Washington Smith, Wallace Neff, Roland E. Coate, Allen Siple, Gordon Kaufmann, John Byers, Paul Williams, Kirtland Cutter, and Carl Lindbom, display a mastery of the wide formal variety found in Spain's rich architectural tradition. From this immense source they could choose such styles as Mudejar or Mozarabic, plateresque or churrigueresque, Italianate classic or *desornamentado.* Among the Spanish models were also variations found in the hilltowns of the Pyrennees, the island of Mallorca, and, especially, the culturally rich province of Andalusia.

Architects often incorporated Mexican, New Mexican, and American colonial elements into the Spanish revival styles, but they viewed indigenous ethnic sources as less desirable and used these less frequently or in minimal form. Today, regional structures and folk art produced by California's natives and settlers are better appreciated. Elements derived from the Native American culture, the Spanish mission-rancho period, the Mexican occupation, and American colonization bring new vitality to houses such as the Culberg House and Casa Callaway.

Contemporary architects and designers also apply a broad, abstract interpretation to Spanish revival design. In the 1960s and 1970s, Charles Moore led the movement to continue California's Spanish "heritage." His style of abstract, overscaled images and forms is seen in the Anawalt House, designed with John Ruble and Robert Yudell. On the other hand, Henry Lenny and Jeffrey Gorrell's Battistone House is a sumptuous but typical example of ornate Spanish style from the 1980s and 1990s. Its overt and detailed imagery appears historicist, but in fact reinterprets Moorish, Mexican, and Italian sources. In contrast, Mexican architect Ricardo Legorreta moves forward into a totally contemporary style in his Greenberg House; it is a distilled form of Mexican peasant houses and Aztec temples, lacking in imagery and ornament except for the rich folk colors and regional landscaping.

The Los Angeles area abounds with Mediterranean- and Spanish-style residences, but the style is especially prevalent in smaller communities like Santa Barbara, where Thomas Bollay, Robert Easton, and James Morris continue to expand the idiom, and in San Diego, where Rob Wellington Quigley abstracts its elements for high-style private houses and public housing (fig. 1).

1. Quigley Apartment, Beaumont Building, San Diego, 1988, Rob Wellington Quigley.

Between 1883 and 1890, when the population of Southern California increased from sixty-four thousand to two hundred thousand, a number of architects were inspired by the mission-rancho period. This claim to the mission background coincided with one of the greatest of American real estate booms. Affluent gringos generated the myth of an indigenous California architecture based on "Spanish roots," an appropriate and visually appealing cultural legend that was useful in selling property in Southern California to eastern investors and midwestern settlers. Between 1910 and 1930, architects expanded on this fictional style, bypassing the Spanish colonial mission tradition to add themes of the Spanish homeland to their sources. The Spanish revival thus brought to Southern California's cities the overall imagery, common names, typological structures, and architectural ideals of Spain.

Late-nineteenth-century architects and real estate promoters both felt that Southern California's true ethnic roots did not provide a marketable architectural tradition. The land was first settled by Native Americans whose impermanent dwellings were made of perishable materials. Beginning in the fifteenth and sixteenth centuries, Spanish and English explorers landed on the Pacific coast and laid claim to the land for their respective monarchs, but it remained occupied by the Native Americans. Spanish colonial culture expanded north from Mexico across the Rio Grande between 1690 and 1836, bringing the Franciscan and Dominican missionaries into the western wilderness, from Texas to California.

In 1769, the king of Spain decided to firm up his claims to California. He sent Father Junipero Serra and a coterie of priests, along with a small body of soldiers, to begin the task of mission building. At that time, a few Spanish settlers, including the younger sons of Spanish grandees, received enormous land grants from Spain. The padres erected chapels, hospices, and administrative buildings in adobe brick and stone. Considering the missionaries' limited technical knowledge, meager tools, and untrained craftsmen, the architectural and decorative results of their labor were astonishing in form and spiritual expression. The missions' pedimented facades, colorful tile-roofed towers, graceful belfries, and cloistered patios created both dramatic silhouettes and symbols of peaceful sanctuary in the untamed California landscape.

Despite the missions' bland exteriors, their interiors were enriched with painted imitations of archaic classical columns, pilasters, and cornice moldings. Roofs and ceilings were usually supported by exposed beams and only occasionally displayed barrel vaults or catenary arches. The decorations were sometimes Moorish-Gothic, plateresque, or exuberant, baroque churrigueresque forms. Sometimes native artisans interpolated motifs of Indian origin that were crude but effective. The mission furniture was simple, sturdily built, and rectangular. Heavily proportioned chairs, chests, tables, and wardrobes were made in native woods joined with mortise, tenon, and dowel. The original furniture that remains shows little relationship to eighteenth-century Spanish detail.

Fifty-two years of Spanish mission settlement ended with the Mexican War of Independence in 1821, when officials in Mexico City declared ownership of all the lands that Spain had claimed. For nearly twenty-five years Mexico struggled to control the Spanish landholders, but with the 1846–48 U.S.-Mexican War, Mexico lost ownership of California. Under the Treaty of Guadaloupe Hidalgo, the United States reached a settlement with Mexico and bought any territories in dispute. Monterey became the capital of the new state of California and, helped by the railroad and the growing system of roads, American settlers imported colonial styles and furnishings from the East, particularly New England. Helen Hunt Jackson provided detailed description of the Spanish rancho and Native American dwellings during this period of American settlement in her 1884 novel *Ramona,* which drew attention to the plight of the Indians who had lost their homes and territorial rights in California's takeover.

Since the mid-nineteenth century, Americans in general had displayed a growing interest in romantic accounts of Spain, from Washington Irving's *Tales of the Alhambra* of 1828 to the range of nineteenth-century Hispanophile literary and musical works. Toward the end of the nineteenth century, art periodicals began showing material from Italy, Spain, Germany, China, Japan, India, and Turkey, which inspired many accurate reproductions of period rooms. In most cases the suitability of the adaptation was of little consideration. However, these periodicals fueled an interest in the appropriateness of Spanish- and Mediterranean-style architecture and furnishings for regions like Florida and Southern California and inspired historians like Austin Whittlesey to spend months in Spain drawing and photographing examples of classical and vernacular architecture. In the preface to Whittlesey's 1917 book *Minor Ecclesiastical, Domestic and Garden Architecture of Southern Spain,* architect Bertram G. Goodhue describes how the Spanish province of Andalusia was discovered by American architects as an important architectural source. Other popular works used for copying Spanish details included A.C. Mitchell's *An Artist in Spain* (1914) and books by Montecito resident George Steedman's friends Mildred Stapley Byne and Arthur Byne: *Spanish Architecture of the Sixteenth Century* (1917), *Spanish Gardens and Patios* (1924), *Provincial Houses in Spain* (1927), and *Majorcan Houses and Gardens* (1928).

David Gebhard's analysis reveals that the Spanish colonial revival occurred in two phases, the mission revival (ca. 1890–1920), and the Mediterranean revival (ca. 1920–1940). During the first phase, using the early mission buildings as their source, California architects developed a new style that contrasted with the over-detailed Queen Anne buildings that continued to be built as late as 1910. Admittedly, the style worked best in larger buildings, such as hotels, train stations, and post offices, where the original scale of the missions could be matched somewhat. These architects borrowed the idea of the mission's undecorated, stuccoed walls and scalloped, parapeted gable-end facades. Their works included elements such as arched openings and loggias, quatrefoil windows, tile roofs, and stepped and/or domed bell towers.

2. Mission Inn (formerly Glenwood Inn), Riverside, 1890–1901, Arthur H. Benton, original architect.

3. California Building (now Museum of Man), Panama-California International Exposition, San Diego, 1915, Bertram G. Goodhue.

Occasionally a centered, parapeted gable was flanked by bell towers, exactly copying the mission facade. Revival architects often added Sullivanesque or Islamic ornament in clearly defined and banded areas. The style was exhibited at Chicago's World Columbia Exposition of 1893, in A. Page Brown's California Building, and one of the best preserved examples still in use is the Mission Inn (formerly the Glenwood Inn) (1890-1901) in Riverside, designed by Arthur H. Benton (fig. 2). The style was often alluded to in the open-beam living rooms of the 1920s Mediterranean houses. By 1900, the mission revival was also related to the American arts and crafts movement. Its residential plans were simple and boxlike, like the Craftsman houses of Gustav Stickley, and the simple furniture the padres had used formed the basis for the popular oak "mission" furniture of the time.

Both the mission compound and the rancho compound derived from a common form, the courtyard house of Spain. Throughout its centuries of Arab rule, Spain developed the basic Greco-Roman form of the patio house that it had inherited from Roman domination. The walled mission compound was a protected building organized around a green space punctuated with a fountain or well and surrounded by arcades, verandas, and porches. On the other hand, the rancho, as the center of a productive livestock-breeding or agricultural complex, was a practical arrangement of introverted residential and service buildings focused on an open courtyard.

In the late teens, the shift from the mission revival to the Mediterranean revival was accompanied by the relaxation of spare Craftsman forms for detailed elaborations befitting the affluent 1920s courtyard houses. Easier to domesticate than the mission revival, Mediterranean revival became the preferred residential style during this period. Numerous examples of what could be described as Spanish colonial revival buildings appeared as early as 1900, but the Mediterranean revival did not really mature until after World War I, reaching its heyday between 1924 and 1932.

Precipitating the Mediterranean revival, Beaux-Arts trained architects arrived on the Southern California scene from eastern schools and European travels. While the traditional grand tour was halted during World War I, Spain remained one of the few European countries available for architectural touring and study. Architects wanted to experience firsthand what the Spanish explorers, padres, and grandees had used as sources for their mission and colonial buildings. They returned to, or settled in, California at a time of commercial expansion, producing erudite copies of many Spanish styles distinguished by specific periods and regions.

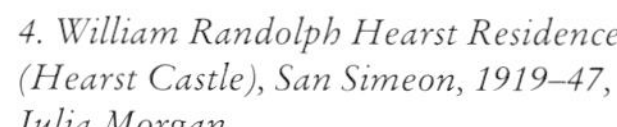

4. William Randolph Hearst Residence (Hearst Castle), San Simeon, 1919–47, Julia Morgan.

5. Los Angeles Times Demonstration House, Pacific Palisades, 1927, Mark Daniels.

The Spanish colonial revival movement received its chief notice at the 1915 Panama-California International Exposition in San Diego (fig. 3). This served the same purpose for the Spanish style in California—to make it popular and fashionable—as had the 1893 World Columbian Exposition in Chicago for neoclassicism in America. In a simplification of the development, Bertram Goodhue and Carleton Winslow, Sr., have often been credited with introducing the eighteenth-century churrigueresque style to California through their exposition buildings. In most cases the style was handled with restraint; it was applied to fewer residential buildings than large public buildings, such as churches, apartment buildings, and stores. One of the best examples is Julia Morgan's house for William Randolph Hearst (Hearst Castle) (fig. 4) in San Simeon (1919–47). The house and its rich architectural details, interiors, and furnishings brought to Southern California a wealth of fifteenth- through nineteenth-century Spanish decorative arts.

Of all the provinces of Spain, it was Andalusia that offered California architects an easily adaptable form that suited the state's climate and landscape. The province includes the cities of Cordoba, Seville, and Granada, and the ports of Cadiz and Malaga; its rich heritage of houses, palaces, and provincial farmhouses provided abundant sources of inspiration. Andalusian farmhouses are traditionally white-stuccoed, sculptural volumes with larger and smaller parts assembled in an informal massing. A limited range of materials—stucco, wood, tile—is accompanied by simple interior and exterior details. An exemplary work of this Andalusian-Spanish style and its relationship of house to garden is the 1927 Los Angeles Times Demonstration House in Pacific Palisades (fig. 5), by architect and landscape architect Mark Daniels, who was an associate of Elmer Grey.

Despite their courtyards and balconies, Spanish colonial revival houses had distinctly separate interiors and exteriors and typical twentieth-century American plans. While the Spanish house was an efficient living space due to the scale of its rooms, revival architects in fact reduced the grand scale in their Spanish-style houses, imparting to them a modest, comfortable appearance. The Spanish plan and the formal vocabulary of its Mediterranean variations also worked well with groups of buildings and planned communities, as well as with city planning and landscaped gardens (fig. 6).

During the Mediterranean phase of the Spanish colonial revival, architects in Southern California produced both literal copies and original transformations. They rarely used exotic Moorish elements in their pure form, preferring to include the Moorish style as a tamer part of a Mudejar or Mozarabic source. They often drew on Italianate elements within the Spanish styles: Renaissance, plateresque, churrigueresque, and classical. Many architects of the 1920s and 1930s blended pure Italian elements and landscape design into otherwise Spanish designs.

6. El Paseo, Santa Barbara, 1921–22, James Osborn Craig with Mary Craig and Carleton Winslow, Sr.

Occasionally, Southern California architects drew certain details and forms from closer to home, such as the adobe folk architecture of colonial California, Mexico, and New Mexico, and the popular American colonial Monterey style—a hybrid of Spanish colonial and New England architecture. For the real estate agents and architects of the late nineteenth and early twentieth century, however, American vernacular did not provide the glamour, mystery, and romance of the missions and Andalusia.

Toward the end of the Mediterranean revival period, from late 1928 through 1929, architects from across the state rallied to rename the movement "California style." These architects were backed by the strength of the Palos Verdes Art Jury, the Santa Barbara Architectural Board of Review, and the Southern California Chapter of the American Institute of Architects. Articles ran in all the local newspapers proclaiming that these boards had approved resolutions to discontinue the use of the terms *mission, Spanish,* or *Mediterranean* in favor of *California style.* Here was recognition that the Spanish colonial revival had produced something other than mere revival, something peculiarly Californian and modern.

Historians quickly acknowledged the unique development. Sheldon Cheney summarized it well in his 1930 book, *The New World Architecture*: "[A] slow moving body of architects . . . gradually settles down to one historic style, the Spanish and its Colonial approximations, as a 'source' . . . in accordance with climatic conditions, available materials and modern use-demands . . . a body of work only very faintly flavored with historical idioms and allusions."

Throughout the Spanish colonial revival a few architects kept the perspective of the modern movement, recognizing that there was something essential and modern in the forms of mission and Spanish architecture that aligned them conceptually with the European secessionist works. Francis Underhill, Frank Mead, Richard Requa, and Irving Gill stripped away historical details to present elemental shapes and forms: arches, cubes, and rectangles. Gill best expressed this view of Spanish vernacular and old mission architecture in his body of work and in his writings. For example, his Women's Club in La Jolla (1927–29) (fig. 7) displays the "long low lines, graceful arcades . . . arched doorways and walled gardens" that he described as part of a Hispanic architecture "retaining tradition, history, and romance."

In a similar manner that perhaps addresses California's true Native American heritage, modernist Rudolph Schindler drew on pueblo designs, and Frank Lloyd Wright and his son Lloyd Wright abstracted modern elements from Mayan and Aztec forms. Santa Monica architect John Byers, however, best expressed the local Mexican roots. He first worked in the adobe tradition of Mexican land grant architecture and even employed a Mexican muralist of the social reform movement to decorate one of his houses.

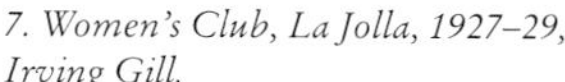
7. Women's Club, La Jolla, 1927–29, Irving Gill.

8. Beverly Hills Civic Center, 1985, Urban Innovations Group/Charles Moore.

Throughout the 1930s and subsequent decades, the Spanish colonial revival declined. The moderne influences of the thirties did much to dilute certain forms into a modern populist format. This was the era of Spanish-deco apartment houses, Hollywood western sets, ranchero furniture, and ceramic crafts from Franciscan and other California potteries. The Southern California Latino community became increasingly active in recognizing and acknowledging problems in racial equality during the 1930s, and it finally caught up with Anglo culture that the recent Spanish colonial revival had little connection to the local Mexican population, the true inheritors of a Spanish colonial past.

In the 1960s and 1970s, when the Chicano movement did much to further educate both Latinos and the general public about the strengths of Latino culture, Charles Moore arrived on the scene and supported a pop abstraction of Spanish design as a fitting association with California's Latino heritage. The late architect's final civic work, the Beverly Hills Civic Center (1985) (fig. 8), is a reminder that the roots, the rich formal variety, and the inclusive nature of the Spanish colonial revival may speak more persuasively to the population of the Los Angeles area in the 1990s than it ever did in the 1920s.

Casa California

SPANISH-STYLE HOUSES FROM SANTA BARBARA TO SAN CLEMENTE

George and Carrie Steedman House

George Washington Smith, *architect*

Now a museum owned by the Casa del Herrero Foundation

Tropical planting provides a thick screen of privacy for the pebble-paved motor court entrance.

Casa del Herrero

MONTECITO, 1922–1925

The pleasure of seasonal visits to Montecito convinced St. Louis residents George and Carrie Steedman and their two daughters to make the community their permanent home in 1930. Steedman had worked in the family business, a metal foundry and equipment manufacturer that prospered with munitions contracts during World War I. In 1922 he bought the land, with views south to the Pacific Ocean and north to the Santa Ynez Mountains. Steedman selected the best-known local architect, George Washington Smith, to build a Spanish-style house on the eleven-acre parcel, which was sparsely covered and crossed by two creeks.

From the outset the house was to be Andalusian in style, and Smith developed four separate schemes before he settled on the final plan. The University of California at Santa Barbara archives retain over two hundred drawings and sketches that Smith made of the house. Steedman and Smith enjoyed their working relationship and often poured over many versions of a detail before making a final decision. The two worked with local landscape designer Ralph Stevens and horticulturalist Peter Reidel.

A wall was built along the entrance road, so the estate is entered indirectly at a corner through several formal enclosures. To the left, a short curving drive leads through a thick screen of trees to a motor court at the entrance to the house. A tiled fountain punctuates the center of the motor court but does not align with the front door, giving the impression of the relaxed symmetries and casual simplicity of the Andalusian farmhouse. Iron grills, also typical of the Andalusian style, ornament and secure each window. The antique Spanish entrance door is made more elaborate and important by its medieval sculpted stone surround crowned with a grilled balcony that opens to the upper stairhall.

Inside, the entrance hall is medieval in style and monasterial in feeling, with many Spanish medieval to early-Renaissance pieces—church chairs, choir stalls, and two *vargueño* cabinets. The key piece is the fifteenth-century painted ceiling of a monastic house from the Convent of San Francisco, near Naranco, in the province of Teruel, once part of Spain's Kingdom of Aragon. It was the largest purchase the Steedmans made on two buying trips to Spain and Portugal. Each purchase was carefully planned for its place in the house or garden and Steedman kept excellent records of provenance. Smith, too, made buying trips to Spain and Mexico and masterfully integrated all of the Steedman purchases into their house.

A corner fireplace with the Steedman crest accents the dining room, which opens broadly to the hallway and the curved staircase that Steedman and Smith resolved after many discussions. Its fine brass finial is one of many metal decorative details that Steedman crafted.

Imported Spanish and European tapestries and antiques give the living room its regal appearance. With the patina of age, the large relief crest on the fireplace appears authentically medieval, until one recognizes the date 1925 prominently displayed below the Sagittarian image of Steedman. Grand as it is, the living room is upstaged by a compelling view of the east garden that is first perceived at the entrance hall. The view continues through the terrace doors of the living room, across the patio and the east garden to an arched, tiled exedra. The east garden is a "room" of planting flanked on the north and south by clipped Eugenia hedges. Behind it is a formal rose garden; beyond that a random grouping of trees forms the background.

Casa del Herrero's principal facade faces the immense south garden at the rear of the house. Here, the central focus is a loggia modeled after the fifteenth-century Villa Cigliano in San Casciano, in the Pesa River valley of Italy. Although its source is Italian rather than Spanish, the loggia fits into the overall Spanish Andalusian structural block.

On the west side of the house, the stone-paved service court outside the kitchen gives the appearance of a working Andalusian farm. Across this court, Steedman built a large workshop where he personally crafted switchplates, finials, sconces, grills, and his trademark garden furniture for the house. A darkroom and winery were added below the workshop.

George Washington Smith died in 1930, and Steedman died only ten years later. Carrie Steedman continued to live in the house until her death in 1963. At that time, their daughter Medora Steedman Bass inherited the house and kept it in a perfect state until her death in 1987. Her son George S. Bass placed the property in trust, then in 1994 he and family members gave the property and all its contents to the Casa del Herrero Foundation to be preserved as a museum. The Foundation, a nonprofit charitable organization, opened the house to the public in 1995. Board members and volunteer docents are now uncovering the Steedmans' sales records and researching the furnishings that make the house an invaluable resource for Hispanic decorative arts.

Left: A fanciful Gothic-style birdhouse, one of several throughout the estate, punctutates the lawn of the south garden.

Opposite: Paved with Tunisian and local tiles, the patio is the first "room" of the east garden reached from the living room through the beaded wooden shutters and down the tiled stairs, right. The owner translated Spanish-style tables and quilted leather chairs into cast aluminum for outdoor use. The freestanding arcade defines the outdoor room and separates it from the south garden.

Above: The loggia of the south facade reflects Italian influence, while Spanish-Moorish garden traditions are the source of the tiled water channel and the garden axis that extends into a series of outdoor rooms.

Right: Toward the end of the water channel is the last garden room, with its scalloped fountain; beyond it, a Spanish iron gate and an aloe plant introduce a sandy desertscape of cactus and succulents. This feature became a popular California variation on the Spanish garden theme.

An ornately tiled exedra fountain is the final focus of the east garden. Beside it, pots, tiled dado, and tiled seating furnish the space.

One of the original owner's favorite areas of the house was the south garden loggia, for which he designed his cast aluminum furniture. Decorative details include the traditional Spanish-Moorish tiled-and-shuttered niche, imported wooden doors, and iron grills and light fixtures. The dado is edged in Moorish tile patterns.

Above: A focal point of the dining room is the open staircase—the picturesque result of a joint decision between architect and client to relate the two spaces.

Opposite: The patina of age is expressed throughout the 1925 house, particularly in the structural design of the entrance hall, with its built-in carved doors and fifteenth-century Spanish ceiling. The choir stalls and vargueño *cabinet, left, are also Spanish imports.*

George Washington Smith, *architect*

Now owned by Casablanca Beach Estates

An exotic tiled entrance portal, a minaret, pointed arches, and a dome match their Moorish forms to California palms as suitable elements for a recreational building type, the indoor pool house, or natatorium.

Isham Beach House Natatorium

SANDYLAND (SANTA BARBARA), 1926

The words *magical* and *dreamlike* are often associated with tales from the *Thousand and One Nights* and appropriately describe the 1926 Isham Beach House Natatorium. The pure white, Moorish-style pleasure pavilion at Sandyland was designed by George Washington Smith for Albert K. Isham, who was known as a flamboyant millionaire playboy. For Isham and several later generations of Santa Barbara socialites the exotic structure has served as a party pavilion for benefits and gala costume balls.

The minaret and bulbous dome that crown the Natatorium, as well as the graceful palms that punctuate the front entrance, can be seen from a distance. The entrance hall, a flat-roofed, one-story wing, projects from the taller pool-house structure. The tile surround that announces the entrance is squared on the outside but forms a Moorish horseshoe arch on the inside around the sturdy, wood double door. This door and the crenellated roofline represent fortresslike elements of the Moorish style.

Architect Smith and his wife traveled and studied in Europe in the 1910s, a time when exotic architecture and artistic themes held sway in the academies there and in America. Smith later settled in Paris for a brief period to study painting at the Julian Academy of the École des Beaux-Arts with American painters George Bellows and Robert Henri. The 1926 Isham design, a result of Smith's travels and education and guided by his romanticism, represents his most painterly and artistic work, yet it is academic and fantastically historicist. During his travels, Smith saw the Alhambra, the last, most exemplary palace constructed by the Moors in Spain. Like a scaled-down version of the Alhambra, which is planned around numerous arcaded courtyards, the Natatorium is covered inside with fantastic and minutely colored ornamental details that are subordinated to the effect of the whole.

The Moors were excellent craftsmen and their castles, palaces, mosques, bazaars, hospitals, and caravansaries display sharp contrast between a plain exterior and an exquisitely ornate interior. This characteristic continued, in permanent form, the tradition of the Moorish nomad's tent, which was richly decorated inside with handwoven textiles and brass lamps.

Smith accurately noted the rich combination of materials in Moorish buildings: colored tiles forming geometric patterns, intricate brickwork, colored plaster ornament in relief, and ornamental leather. Floor tiles of varied patterns express the floor plan, and wall friezes contain running geometric motifs of intersecting polygons, stars, and crosses. The brilliant primary hues of the tilework, plaster ornament, painted woodwork, and rich wool textiles were inherited from the Moors' nomadic forebears.

Not all the Moorish decorative elements and materials are seen at the Natatorium, but Smith's "Moorish" details are unmistakable, including the horseshoe arch. This structural form was used by the Visigoths, but it is generally thought to have been introduced independently by the Moors, although both groups may have inherited it from the Romans. Inside the Natatorium the three-quarter arches spring directly from a column capital to define a poolside living room. The octagonal columns are short in order to support the large, high, horseshoe openings and are clad with colorful, patterned tiles. The capitals are square and covered with solid green tiles in conventional motifs. Woodwork, as in Moorish structures, is limited to the doors and the ceiling.

Smith knew that the Koran prohibited the representation of the human form, so he used a rich geometry of stars, crescents, crosses, hexagons, and octagons for the decorative work at the Natatorium. However, the Islamic Shi'a sect was always more tolerant of human and animal figures and produced them to the great displeasure of the Sunni sect. Therefore, Smith freely chose what he felt most appropriate.

He surrounded the fireplace in the south poolside living room with a lyrical scene based on Persian miniatures, with ladies and their attendant servants in a lush garden. At the opposite end of the pool, another tile mural depicts an underwater fantasy, while the tiled wainscot of the poolside resembles a Persian carpet.

Smith's only Moorish design was this Natatorium, and in fact, this is the only truly Moorish-style structure in Southern California from the period. Nonetheless, Smith's stylistic preference and that of the majority in the 1920s California movement remained Andalusian.

Below: One corner of the Moorish-style interior shows the elaborate interlaced tilework used for wainscoting, the framed niche for the water fountain, and the octagonal column.

Opposite: Octagonal columns and horseshoe arches define a poolside living room. The lofty space is tripartite, with vaulted ceilings and hanging brass lamps.

Tile wainscoting emphasizes the large 20′ by 60′ space of the Natatorium. Above, the retractable ceiling is supported by a dropped wood soffit with artesonado *ornament, the carved woodwork that provides a broad crowning element to the space. At the far end, a fireplace and wicker chairs furnish the poolside living room.*

Above: Persian miniatures depicting lyrical garden scenes were the source for the tile mural above the fireplace in the poolside living room.

Opposite: A pattern of wood moldings and hammered-and-tooled bronze hardware decorates the Natatorium's Moorish-style doors.

Henry Lenny and Jeffrey Gorrell of Sharpe, Mahan and Lenny, *architects*

The central tower and picturesque stone carving and grillwork of this contemporary hillside Spanish-Moorish house is best appreciated from the motor court. A curved double stair leads down to the entrance court.

Battistone House

HOPE RANCH, SANTA BARBARA, 1991

How does one design a traditional Spanish-Moorish-style house in California in the 1990s? Roger and Cristina Battistone gave architect Henry Lenny the opportunity to answer that question only a few years ago. "Cristina and I had traveled in southern Spain," says Roger. "We stayed at old paradors—castles and church retreats—and went to the Alhambra. That's the architecture I really like. And when it came to designing our new house, I felt something traditionally Spanish was appropriate for Santa Barbara." Lenny, a perfect candidate to provide the Battistones with a historicist point of view, is a member of Santa Barbara's Historic Landmarks Commission, and at the time, he had just finished restoring Santa Barbara's El Paseo, a courtyard structure from the 1920s that now houses shops, restaurants, and offices.

Seen from the entrance drive or the adjacent golf course, the terra-cotta-colored walls, central tower, wrought iron balconies and Moorish-arched windows and doors set the stage for a fairy-tale version of a Spanish-Moorish manor house. After Lenny had completed the conceptual sketches and William Rivera had worked on the preliminary drawings, Jeffrey Gorrell became involved. "My job was to expand on Lenny's design," explains Gorrell. "The house begins with a central mass that holds the stair tower, the entrance hall, and the living room. Then a U-shaped configuration encloses the front entrance court—the Spanish always made a celebration out of the entrance. The split stair comes down the hill to the house, which has a balcony, a stone door surround, and a wrought iron and glass door. From the focal point of the living room and entrance hall you look back out to the tiled fountain and the curving stairs going up the hill on either side." On the inside of the curved stair wall, facing the front door, is a grand peacock fountain that is based freely on the one made by Malibu Potteries for the historic Adamson House (p. 56).

Like an interior courtyard, the living room is down a few steps, through the Moorish horseshoe arches. On one side an interior window opens to the upper dining room. The wall of arcaded terrace doors, the garden urns filled with exotic plants, and the raised sandstone fireplace create an outdoor feeling typical of a Spanish courtyard-living room.

James Lasseter, who designed the interiors, helped with finishes, colors, and window types. "I was trying to keep it in the 1920s model that Lenny had started with," says Lasseter. "For the pools and fountains and interior details, I researched Malibu Tile and looked at original artwork. The tiles are true to original Malibu Tile colors, but I avoided oranges and yellows."

The interior is reminiscent of the Palace of the Marques de Dos Aguas (1744) in Valencia, Spain, where the baroque style was expressed by elaborate wall frescoes showing floral and tropical vegetation, distorted architectural forms in plaster, gilded stucco cartouches, heraldic motifs, and exaggerated door and window trim. Many of the palace's walls are of sand-finished plaster left a natural color, which accentuates the brilliancy of the drapery and cushion materials. Parquetry, inlaid floor patterns, and beamed or frescoed ceilings complete the interiors. Similar decorative elements are found throughout the Battistone House.

"I've found so many different inspirations for the Spanish style," says Lasseter. "I interpreted the furniture as country-made formal furniture. The pieces are not overly refined, but definitely for the manor house, like examples of a village craftsman's best work." They are influenced by the Italian artists, architects, and craftsmen who traveled to Spain in the sixteenth and seventeenth centuries and by local craftsmen who added regional variations and character.

Leading from the motor court and garage wing, the double stair curves around the entrance court fountain and reflection pool in the form of a terra-cotta stucco wall with slender wrought iron railing.

Above: Tilework, modeled on many of the forms and colors produced by the historic Malibu Potteries, surrounds a fountain on the terrace that looks out to the entrance courtyards through arabesque horseshoe arches.

Right: A stepped tile wall fountain with mixed and matched tile patterns constantly trickles water into the swimming pool. Above the pool terrace, the house rises up the hill; the Moorish-style stone balustrades of the living room terrace and master bedroom balcony add fortresslike strength to the design.

Right: One of the children's bedrooms features a low, pointed-arch window with an interior wooden shutter. Piles of pillows on the daybed add to the exotic "caravansary" mood of the fanciful mural depicting a desert landscape seen through drapery swags and a pointed arch.

Below: Pink limestone is used in the sunken living room for the paired columns, pierced balustrades, and raised fireplace.

Opposite: An ornate balcony with robustly carved brackets projects into the entrance hall. The Spanish baroque-style staircase is richly tiled and ornamented with a wrought iron railing and an architectural mural by Kurt Venner depicting turbaned Moorish figures.

Schneider House

Former Samuel Knight House

George Washington Smith and Lutah Maria Riggs, *architects*

Cleo Baldon, *renovation and landscape architect*

Andalusian farmhouses inspired the simple but stately white-stuccoed facade facing the broad motor court.

Casa de Buena Vista

MONTECITO, 1929–1935

When George Washington Smith designed and built his own Andalusian-style house in 1916 in Montecito, he established the essence of his highly abstract design approach, and the house proved to be the springboard for his career as the area's leading Spanish-revival architect.

He developed the abstract front wall of his house in other designs such as the Osthoff House (1924) in Pasadena and this house, Casa de Buena Vista, formerly the Samuel Knight House. As seen in the Knight House, the long entrance wall is simple and even severe, with a row of grilled windows on the low, one-story wing. The main, double-story rectangular mass is uninterrupted except by the entrance door, a simple grilled balcony with French doors above it, and the grilled window of an interior stairway in the middle of the facade. The typical Spanish entrance door surround is absent; instead, there is only an upper tile panel and side tiles set flush to the wall.

Casa de Buena Vista is named for one of the streets that borders its seven-and-a-half-acre landscaped site. A Monterey balcony and a U-shaped courtyard at the rear of the house overlook this setting. Throughout the house the decorative elements are characteristically broad and planar, such as a wide, unadorned outdoor fireplace facing the courtyard and a similar one in the living room. The current residents have expanded on this sense of breadth and united two children's bedrooms into one large master bedroom that opens onto the Monterey balcony.

"We bought the house about thirteen years ago," says owner Margie Schneider. "Nobody had lived here for ten years, so it was our mission to put it back to the way it had been. We didn't want to spoil the integrity because we liked all the details, the beams, even the rusted front gate." The house had some rooms that only could have been built in the 1920s, including a hidden dry bar put in during Prohibition. There was a butler's pantry with a safe for the silver and a walk-in safe in the basement, now used as the wine cellar. Recently, designer Cleo Baldon remodeled the kitchen, adding a greenhouse breakfast niche, and reconfigured the master suite. She also added a pool and expanded the rear courtyard to create a formal, classical balustraded terrace that overlooks the garden.

In 1921, architect Smith hired Lutah Maria Riggs as a draftsman, shortly after she had graduated from the University of California at Berkeley. Riggs thoroughly understood Smith's work and later became his associate; in 1929, the year the Knight House was commissioned, Smith began discussing a full partnership with her. However, before that could take place, Smith died suddenly of a heart attack. Riggs finished construction of the house, made some alterations to it between 1932 and 1933, and formed a partnership with Harold Edmondson to finish Smith's work and continue his practice.

Right: Architect George Washington Smith enriched the flat facades of the house with a variety of Spanish-style window grills, some of which were acquired on his trips to Spain and Mexico.

Below: A driveway leading to the motor court passes a long, one-story wing of the house, accentuated by grilled windows and topiary.

A wall of traditional square-paned windows opens the dining room to the sprawling seven-and-a-half acre site.

At the rear of the house, the U-shaped courtyard is framed by one-story wings. Here, Smith included relatively modern forms—a wide squared fireplace and chimney, an unadorned Monterey balcony, and broad-paned French doors.

Left: A tiled Adoration of the Magi scene on one courtyard wall is typical of the subjects depicted by Spanish tilemakers working in an Italianate style.

Opposite, above: The Italian chandelier in the dining room is a recent addition, as is the stenciled border around the windows, designed in the Spanish style.

Left: In 1935, a few years after the house was completed, Riggs completed its most notable feature, the library. This wood-paneled, spacious addition to the west wing extends the house into the side garden. The entire room and its details, like the ornate overmantel and window shutters, are superb examples of Moorish moderne woodwork.

Merritt and Rhoda Adamson House

Stiles O. Clements, *architect, of Morgan, Walls & Clements*

Now the Malibu Lagoon Museum

The beach side of the house features a U-shaped courtyard and balcony with Moorish-tiled side wings.

Adamson House

MALIBU, 1928

For one young couple in Southern California during the mid-1920s, Spanish-style architecture was very nearly an inescapable choice for their house. Both Merritt Huntley Adamson and Rhoda Rindge Adamson were from California founding families: Rhoda was the daughter of Frederick Hastings Rindge and Rhoda May Rindge, who were among the last inheritors of the Malibu Spanish land grant. Spanish architecture had personal meaning for Rhoda; she grew up surrounded by themes of the Spanish pioneers and listening to tales her father, a California ranchero, recorded in his 1898 book, *Happy Days in Southern California*.

The Adamsons chose a picturesque site for the house, Vaquero Hill, where Malibu Creek meets the ocean. The house is on a small rise overlooking the ocean and Malibu Lagoon, an inlet and bird sanctuary. In 1927 the Adamsons asked architect Stiles O. Clements to design the house. He had developed a moderne style based on revival themes, but prior to this work, he was not known for traditional Spanish design. Only four years before the Adamson commission, he formed the partnership of Morgan, Walls & Clements, a Los Angeles architecture and engineering firm which, over the years, was noted for modern commercial work. At the flagstone motor court entrance, Clements gave the white-stucco, tile-roofed house a simple farmhouse appearance. The facade is a diminutive one-and-a-half stories high with medieval elements, such as the slightly cantilevered upper floor and the projecting stair tower with lead-framed, bottle-glass windows.

On the opposite side of the house, a more elaborate facade looks to the ocean. This facade is more formal due to the symmetry of the U-shaped plan, and exotic Moorish forms and colorful decoration enrich the design. The two side wings are flat-roofed, one-story Moorish pavilions with tile-clad fronts and pointed Moorish-arch windows.

Tiles throughout the house were produced by Malibu Potteries, a family-owned company a half-mile away. Rhoda Adamson's mother, May Rindge, founded the pottery in 1926, in part to provide tiles for her daughter's houses. Malibu Potteries used clay from the nearby hills and was a prolific producer of colorful, handmade Mediterranean-style and Spanish-style ceramicwork and tiles. Although the company operated for little more than a decade, Malibu tiles decorate numerous domestic and commercial buildings throughout Southern California.

In the Adamson House, Spanish- and Moorish-style tiles cover door and window facings, window jambs and seats, step risers, and fountains. They are used at the front door surround, on the chimney, and on some exterior walls and windows. Most Malibu tiles have conventional floral designs covered with an enamel glaze or luster. However, in the Adamson kitchen, the tiles have an abstract, Native American geometric pattern and a color scheme of blue, orange, and black. Each of the five bathrooms in the house is fully tiled in a different pattern and color scheme. The entrance loggia features a majestic *cuerda seca* Persian tile "rug" with fringe in casual disarray. It was created by potter William E. Handley, one of the most talented designers for Malibu Potteries.

Outside the house, tilework animates the landscape and is part of the overall garden design, the pool, and the adjoining bath-house. A flagstone pathway informally winds through the property, yet each fountain is formal and symmetrical, such as the freestanding Moorish star-shaped fountain and the peacock fountain with its heraldic birds along the courtyard wall.

The courtyard's undulating loggia ceiling is decorated with intertwined animal and floral motifs created by Danish artists Ejnar Hansen and Peter Nielsen. The interior design includes hand-carved teakwood doors, molded and wood-beamed ceilings, and hand-wrought filigree ironwork. The furniture throughout is in the Spanish style, and although antiques were used, many pieces were designed or reproduced under the direction of interior designer John Holtzclaw. The house is now owned by the state of California and open to the public as the Malibu Lagoon Museum.

Tiles from the family-owned Malibu Potteries decorate the outer courtyard wall with Spanish-Moorish peacock imagery. Beyond is Malibu Lagoon and Surfrider Beach.

Above: Grape vine-patterned wrought iron grills fill the glazed openings of the courtyard loggia.

Right: Danish artists Ejnar Hansen and Peter Nielsen added a Scandinavian flavor to their decorations on the fireplace hood and ceiling beams in the tile-paved living room. At right, the floor-to-ceiling pointed arch window looks out to the ocean.

Opposite: Inside the loggia entrance hall, a Persian-design tile "rug," an interior window grill, and a vaulted ceiling add Old World charm.

The dining room is furnished with a Spanish-style credenza and studded leather Renaissance-style chairs, and the soffited ceiling is accented with gold leaf for a regal effect.

Above: Adding to the exotic character of the house, Arabic script is incorporated into the design of the Persian wall hanging in the entrance hall.

Right: For the kitchen, tiles were designed in bright hues and geometric forms in an interpretation of local Chumash Indian patterns and colors.

Moore Ruble Yudell, *architects*

At the west end of the beachside terrace, an overscaled wall forms a partial sunscreen and pergola. Simple elements such as pots, arches, and tile paving add to the modern interpretation of the Spanish colonial house.

Anawalt House

MALIBU, 1979

In 1976, Charles Moore wrote that to make architecture useful it "must be the creation of place. . . . To make a place is to make a domain that helps people know where they are and by extension who they are." Moore's work is contemporary and innovative, but he heartily believed in the Spanish style for California. In fact, his Faculty Club (1967) at the University of California at Santa Barbara and Burns House (1974) in Santa Monica Canyon both have been likened good-naturedly to a blend of traditional Mexican architecture and thin Hollywood-lot structures. Together with his Los Angeles partners Robert Yudell and John Ruble, Moore had a particular interest in honoring California's grass-roots tradition of the Spanish style. However, they had not had the opportunity to build in that style until 1978, when David Anawalt came to them for a modern Spanish house.

David Anawalt had been given family property, a two-and-a-third-acre cliffside site on Point Dume in Malibu that was overgrown with native plants in its small canyons and furrows and had its own small sandy cove. Anawalt had lived in Spain for a while and was impressed with the architecture on the Costa Brava north of Barcelona. "I thought Spanish architecture would be suitable for my site," he said, "and I was drawn also to the mission influence in Southern California." He began seeking architects working in the Hispanic tradition, and when he saw the work of the Mexican modernist Luis Barragan in Mexico, he decided to follow that direction. "But I was also looking at oceanfront architecture, and you can't not be fascinated by Sea Ranch." This coastal community in Northern California was designed by MLTW/Moore Turnbull (Charles Moore with Donlyn Lyndon, William Turnbull, and Richard Whittaker) in the 1960s. "That got me into Charles Moore's office and off we went," adds Anawalt. "I told them I wanted a house that looked like one by Luis Barragan at Sea Ranch."

The overall design is thoroughly modern. Its simple lines and squared, sloped, and octagonal shapes contrast and balance in a strong cubist manner. The sculptural qualities are best recognized from the west, where a small canyon filled with native chaparral and imported eucalyptus and olive trees separates the house from its neighbors. "Although Buzz Yudell was the partner we worked with most, Charles Moore came to the site several times and I took him down that small canyon," recalls Anawalt, "and I think the west view of the house just might not have been as dramatic if I hadn't taken Charles out there."

Spanish design elements appear in both conventional and abstracted ways, but following tradition, the house is pink stucco with white wood trim and a tile roof. The entrance courtyard is decorated with an ornate Mexican fountain with water trickling from a sculpted pineapple into a basin supported by three mermaids. There is a loggia on one side of the courtyard and, on the other side, French doors open to an iron balcony.

There are loggias, terra-cotta tile floors, and thick walls with window seats inside, too, but the abstracted and exaggerated Spanish-Mexican forms betray the house's modern roots. Instead of arches, the courtyard's outer wall is composed of clean-lined, trabeated openings that capture Barragan's planar style. His influence is also visible on the west side of the house, where a lofty freestanding wall, also with trabeated openings, protects this facade from direct sunlight and supports an arbor. On the south terrace, other exaggerated architectural forms dominate. Here, the roof plane soars to the height of the octagonal tower of the dining room, below, and master bedroom, above. Although it echoes a medieval form, the tower gives the impression of a modern Spanish colonial fortress looming large over its cliffside site.

The landscaping is informal, tropical, exotic, and lush, with a stand of bamboo, fan palms, and several other varieties of palms at the entrance courtyard. Tall palms grace the living room and the double-height solarium adjacent to it; Anawalt cultivates rare tropical species.

The rooms and corridors of the house are higher and wider on the south, ocean side, so there are actually few right angles in the house. The living room is surrounded by rooms at different floor levels—the kitchen, dining room, study, and solarium. "The house was actually designed as a series of three courtyards," says Anawalt, "with the motor court, the garden courtyard, and the living room, which we also consider a third courtyard."

Below: The tower is an exaggerated element dominating the south facade overlooking a Point Dume cove. It is freely derived from Spanish sources. The arcade walls and angled shed roof are forms typical of Spanish-Mexican ranchos.

Opposite: The west pergola casts its afternoon shadow on the arcadelike glazed openings to the living room, which is treated as an interior courtyard.

Above: In the traditional Spanish-style courtyard at the entrance, a fountain with a basin held by mermaids is offset by a long arcaded walkway.

Right: At one side of the entrance courtyard, a series of clean-lined, post-and-lintel openings lends a modern aspect to the Spanish ambiance.

Opposite: From the entrance porch window, the ocean can be seen beyond the west terrace.

Above: A wall of windows opens one side of the interior courtyard/living room to the ocean view. The built-in window banquettes, tall palms, and tile floor add to the casual courtyard atmosphere. Beyond the arch, steps lead up to the dining room in the lower level of the projecting tower.

Former hunting lodge

Original architect unknown

Carl Day, *renovation architect*

Doug and Regula Campbell, *pool house and landscape architects*

The entrance to the house is in the stone tower, right, a form typical of Spanish colonial revival houses. To the left is an enclosed garden room, the former open porch of the hacienda-style hunting lodge.

Culberg House

SANTA MONICA MOUNTAINS, 1928

In 1928, a hunting lodge was built on a remote 360-acre site in the Santa Monica mountains as retreat for a successful stockbroker. The main house is in the far reaches of a canyon, nestled among the trees at the uppermost portion of the site. It is constructed of indigenous stone, and with its low, red-tiled roof, the house captures the essence of the California vernacular rancho and blends into the wild surroundings. "They blasted the mountain near here to get the rocks and brought them to the site on horse-drawn lorries," explains Leah Culberg, who has owned the ranch house with her husband, Paul, and their two daughters since 1975.

The house was rebuilt and renovated after it was largely destroyed in the devastating 1978 Agoura fire, and the site, now ten acres, includes a guest house, pool, and gardens. All that remained of the house was its foundation and the stone and concrete walls. Despite the trauma of losing their home, the Culbergs wanted to rebuild it and recapture the unique character of the hunting lodge at this idyllic mountain site.

The original structure was unpretentious Spanish colonial revival vernacular with natural-finish exterior walls, a large courtyard, and undecorated interior finishes. "It was possibly influenced by the arts and crafts movement as it was popularized in California by architects such as the Greene brothers and Irving Gill," says architect Carl Day, who rebuilt and renovated the house. "In the 1890s and early 1900s such architects produced numerous houses that were published in the influential journal *The Craftsman*." This house seems to be inspired by El Alisal (1898–1910) in Highland Park, built by Charles F. Lummis, who founded the Landmarks Club, the Southwest Museum, and the journal *The Land of Sunshine* in his efforts to preserve California's Spanish missions and early Native American culture.

What clearly remains unchanged is the original stone-faced courtyard. "The courtyard home provided security in the wilderness while giving a restful, introspective character to the house," says Day. The hunting lodge has a U-shaped plan that forms a 1,300-square-foot outdoor living room enclosed by a six-foot-high garden wall on the open, south side. "The basic plan approximates Vitruvius's axiom that an atrium courtyard house should have the proportions of the Golden Section of three to five," adds Day.

The courtyard actually creates an excellent microclimate. The thick stone walls reduce the sun's glare and provide insulation. The pond cools the air by evaporation, and the outdoor fireplace cuts the chill of Southern California's evenings. Bedrooms, doors, and windows, which can be left open at night, have direct access to the courtyard; on hot summer nights one could sleep there under the stars.

The original interior—with a small kitchen, a single bath, and two bedrooms— cramped the growing family. The kitchen was enlarged and the porch was enclosed with casement windows to create a garden room. Yet additional room was still needed. To avoid any alteration to the classic courtyard plan, Day's solution was to add two bedrooms below the bedroom wing, accessed by a new interior, skylighted circular stairwell. "Except for the hardwood treads, the stairwell materials were all pre-fire," says Paul Culberg. "The main post was a dead Monterey pine and the railing was made from its branches. The risers were fir rafters that survived the disaster; they had caved in under the roof tile so they were actually kiln-hardened in the fire."

Day's completed renovations doubled the original area, and, of course, he placed special emphasis on fire-retardant elements. The new framing eliminated all exterior overhangs; wood balconies were replaced with open steel grating. The new garden room and atrium were also fireproofed. The Culbergs' fine collection of Hickory and California Monterey furniture dates from the period of the original house, according to Leah, who got her first pieces of Hickory at a swap meet.

In 1992, the Culbergs added a pool house/guest suite, swimming pool, spa, and gardens designed by the husband-and-wife team of Doug and Regula Campbell, whose work was sympathetic to the original house. The Campbells reordered the entire hillside site through an interlocking series of patios, terraces, and gardens connected by winding earthen paths and stone stairs. Most characteristic of the rugged setting and the individualistic rancho style, however, is the lower lilac and rose garden. It is highlighted by a rustic *glorieta*—a playful gazebo built of indigenous stone and red manzanita branches draped in fragrant vines.

The pool and pool house were carefully sited to take full advantage of the spectacular mountain views. The bunkhouse form with a breezeway is similar to those of early California ranchos.

Above: During the summer, the owners frequently dine in the U-shaped courtyard. The circular table was made by the owner with patchwork tile. Its pedestal base is a deodora cedar trunk from a tree lost in a 1978 fire. Under the portal overhang is a 1950s Hickory bench in the low-slung, western style.

Opposite: The brick-paved, L-shaped garden room was formerly an open veranda with the same rock walls as the exterior of the house. The original windows, which faced the porch, were moved to the outer walls. An old Hickory table with cane chairs is for casual dining.

Left: The stone-surfaced fireplace is the focus of the wood-beam living room, with furnishings suitable to a hunting lodge—a Victorian horn chair and ottoman, a deer-foot lamp, and a Colfax chaise lounge with two-tone cane weaving. In front of the sofa is a nineteenth-century hammered copper German chest.

Above: A stone fireplace with mantel trimmed in Malibu-style tiles fills one corner of the kitchen; on the right, French doors open to the courtyard. A large 1940s Monterey hutch holds an array of Bauer pottery. The chandelier above the glass-topped dining table was made by the owner from antlers found at swap meets.

Thomas and Claire Callaway House

Thomas Callaway and James Chuda, *renovation architects*

A barnlike workroom, reached through horseshoe-crowned Dutch doors, and a home office face into the courtyard from the rear of the lot. On the left is a 1920s bungalow remodeled in the 1980s with a mix of Spanish colonial, Indian, Mexican, and Anglo elements recalling earlier periods.

Casa Callaway

WEST LOS ANGELES, 1920s

The Callaway House is a case study in the ethnic diversity of the Spanish colonial period, which was characterized by a combination of Native American, Mexican, Spanish, New England, and European tastes. Not historically true to one particular period, the house reflects instead the early Spanish colonial hacienda esthetic, with the craftsmanship and detailing that would have been found in the eclectic home of a well-to-do European settler, a Mexican or American ranchero, or a Mexican-Spanish viceroy or governor.

Thomas Callaway, a transplanted midwesterner who now designs interiors and furniture, and his actress-wife, Claire, found the house—a tiny, shingle-roofed, stucco bungalow—in 1986. The dark, one-bedroom house was built in the 1920s on property that was once part of a Spanish land grant. Callaway was attracted to it for its simplicity and because it was virtually untouched. At the rear of the lot, a ramshackle nineteenth-century adobe brick wall, a remnant of a huge Spanish colonial ranch, sparked Callaway's imagination and became the starting point for his dream rancho. Today, the Callaways' antique-filled hacienda truly creates the Spanish colonial atmosphere of California. The couple has collected an abundance of English and American antiques over many years and Callaway put them to use to produce his vision of a "Spanish-Victorian closet."

Together with architect James Chuda, Callaway set about to enlarge the 1,000-square-foot house. A second floor was added to the old barn at the rear of the lot for a guest suite, home office, and work-room. At the front of the house, they built a new dining/kitchen area. Originally the house ended in a dark, tiny bedroom off the living area; this was knocked through to add bedrooms along a skylit hallway that faces out to a large pool courtyard. The old shake roof was eliminated and replaced with tiles from Saltillo, Mexico, and the house was painted a peachy terra-cotta color with weathered, powder-blue wood trim. Eighteenth-century Argentine ironwood frames and grills open the front dining/kitchen addition with curved, segmented arched windows.

Vigas—the log roof supports used in Native American and Southwest Spanish architecture—uphold the portal, or Spanish veranda, that runs along the courtyard facade. Here, Callaway distressed the windows and French doors to the bedrooms and den to fit the architectural design and antique furnishings. Clearly, Callaway's favorite room is a small den where both the rugged architecture and the furniture come from the land: above, the stucco ceiling is supported by peeled-log beams, and tables and hide-covered chairs are made from twigs, branches, and reeds. The small room is layered with Native American and Western artifacts from floor to ceiling.

The urban rancho is truly complete with the downstairs workroom and its impressive assortment of tools, including saws and implements left to Callaway by Claire's father. "My own father still needs his tools. He's in the trade known as patternmaking, which is a very extraordinary form of woodworking in one of the steps of the foundry trade," says Callaway, who inherited his father's practical innovation and meticulous craftsmanship. "He knows how to build just about anything, and I grew up in the midst of that."

Below: Meals are prepared on the tiled counter in the outdoor cantina and taken on the Mexican table with round pigskin top and intertwined willow base. The chairs were designed for a 1940s western film.

Right: Along the paved portal are distressed windows and French doors, and a weathered plant stand at the end displays a collection of Mexican tin lanterns.

Adirondack chairs accent the courtyard. Viga posts support the portal that the owner added to the side of the original bungalow. Its rooms are reoriented along the skylighted hallway to face out through French windows and doors to the courtyard.

Left: A fountain made from antique Pueblo tiles, with spouts from old French roof ridge ornament, fills the tile-paved entrance courtyard with the sound of trickling water.

Below: In the living room, painted a warm goldenrod color, the owners combined their collection of English and American antiques with Spanish furniture and Mexican and Indian folk art to reflect an eclectic, Spanish colonial hacienda esthetic. Notable pieces include a Spanish colonial santos cupboard on top of a Mexican trestle table, and, above the adobe fireplace, an early-nineteenth-century American portrait.

Opposite: On one side of the entrance courtyard, the door leads into the dining/kitchen addition.

Above: Combining the dining and kitchen area and placing the kitchen prominently at the front of the house reflects the modest approach taken to the whole design. A rancho feeling is introduced by the adobe fireplace and the Mexican worktable used for dining, with its willow-and-leather Mexican chairs.

Opposite: In the kitchen area, brightly colored earthenware and naive religious paintings decorate a distressed painted cupboard flanked by two antique Spanish chairs.

Allen Siple, *architect*

Architect Allen Siple's 1931 design for the house made ample use of its suburban lot. A Moorish-style balcony overlooks the courtyard formed by a compact, L-shaped plan where the one-story living room wing creates the traditional portal arcade, here facing sideways into the space.

Anderson House

WESTWOOD, 1931

In Westwood, developer Edward Janss' popular Spanish- and English-style houses were generally designed by a stable of talented architects, such as Wallace Neff, Gordon Kaufmann, P. P. Lewis, and Allen Siple. The Andersons' Spanish-style house was designed by Siple, who achieved a fine reputation in Los Angeles residential design and whose own Craftsman-style, boulder-rock home in Mandeville Canyon has become a local landmark.

"Nina and I bought the house four years ago after a lengthy search for a good-sized Spanish house with as much of the original tilework and detail as possible," says Peter Anderson. "Most Spanish-style houses don't have their original tiled bathrooms and kitchens. This one did and it had larger rooms than most." The real estate listing called it an "Art Deco Spanish house" and its 1930s date accounts for its larger-scaled rooms, greater attention to amenities such as bathrooms and closets, and angular decorative details. The courtyard house is on a narrow lot and has an economical, L-shaped plan. A two-story wing faces a courtyard on one side and the single-story living room wing on the other. At the juncture of the two wings is a subtly detailed stair tower and an ornately carved wood balcony that overlooks the courtyard.

At the front, a low, overgrown wall defines the courtyard, so the house is entered only through a pair of lacy wrought iron driveway gates on the left or through a T-shaped tiled opening to the courtyard portal on the right. Blue-and-yellow tilework here and throughout the house appears to be inspired by Malibu Tile, with patterns that include heraldic peacocks and Moorish-style interlace.

Light was better appreciated in the 1930s than previously and it is one of the qualities that Nina cherishes most in the house. At the front, a large vertical picture window is framed by a frilly window grill that looks like a balcony at its base. Another large window gives a view of the courtyard fountain from the dining room, and French windows and doors open both the living room and dining room to the shady portal arcade and garden.

The house was carefully detailed, and the Andersons were fortunate that the prior owners had made few alterations. In fact, they may have been responsible for enriching the interiors beyond Siple's original design. "I have rarely seen a house with so much detail," says Peter. "It has great windows, stenciling, and friezes, and original fixtures such as sconces and chandeliers. The bedrooms had textured plaster in a comb pattern and my daughter's bedroom had a rainbow gradation in the plaster, from green to pink. These details aren't Spanish, but terrific design from the 1930s."

Mary Ann Jordan designed the interiors and restored the stencil and tilework where necessary. "We put it all back to the original," she says, "and in every room we had enough of the original to know what to do. All the interior friezes, tilework, and fixtures have very definite deco patterns." The art deco fixtures and detailing set the theme for the furnishings. "We acquired many art deco pieces but we've also included some art nouveau and a few Craftsman works," she continues. "We stayed within the period of the turn of the century through the 1930s." In the living room are two splendid curved-arm American art deco sofas, and the dining room contains a French art deco table and sideboard. Carpets here and in the living room are Chinese art deco made in the 1920s and 1930s strictly for export. Nina's 1940s lamps flank a sumptuous Italian art deco bed.

One addition to the house, a cantina from the 1940s or 1950s, is furnished with Mexican and western furniture and used as an outdoor living room. "It had a bar with a counter and stools," explains Nina, "but we made it into a typical Mexican cantina, with ranchero-style and fleamarket furniture also from the forties and fifties."

A broad, three-part, floor-to-ceiling living room window looks out to the courtyard portal. The owners have furnished the room with American art deco furniture and a Chinese art deco carpet.

POTTERY
BEACH HOUSES

Below: The main entrance to the house is through a T-shaped tiled opening that leads through an ornate iron gate to the courtyard portal.

Right: The rear garden includes an informal cantina, a form derived from either commercial Mexican sources or the protected gathering areas of the vaqueros on the Mexican rancho compound. It is furnished with Mexican and western rancho-style furniture from the 1940s and 1950s.

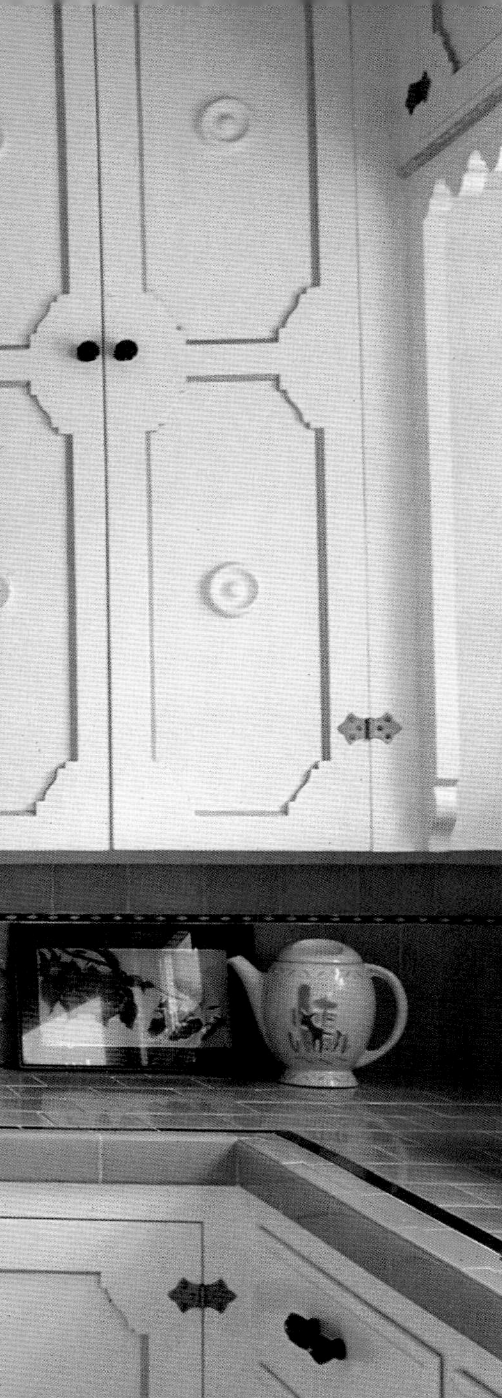

Left: Cabinetry in the kitchen is a simplified version of antique Spanish woodwork in bright colors typical of the 1930s.

Below: The breakfast room's fretwork cabinets are filled with 1930s glassware, and on the counter are pitchers from a collection of California pottery from the 1930s to 1950s—much of which was inspired and developed from the Spanish techniques and Mexican shapes brought to California during the colonial era.

Ellen M. Johnson, *architect*

Barbara Schnitzer, *renovation architect*

Bougainvillea and other plants common to California nearly obscure the view of a 1929 Spanish colonial revival Monterey-style house that is continually being renovated and refined by its current residents. The low courtyard wall with an arched gate is just one recent addition.

Stern and Milch House

BRENTWOOD, 1929

There was nothing unusual about the handsome Spanish-style house in Brentwood that television producer and writer David Milch and painter Rita Stern bought in the mid-1980s. The 1929 house was designed and built by its first owner, Ellen M. Johnson. It has a straightforward Monterey balcony and in plan turns sideways to a courtyard to make the most of its site. Yet the bougainvillea is extremely picturesque, the courtyard is quaint, and the interior is now in a Spanish style updated to the 1990s.

"I worked on it in 1989 after David and Rita finished updating the wiring and plumbing and generally cleaning it up," says interior designer Jarrett Hedborg, who brought in artist Nancy Kintisch to collaborate on the design. Hedborg had worked with Kintisch on earlier projects and appreciated her unusual talent for wall stenciling and choosing colors and materials. In the living room, the designers enhanced the lofty, missionlike structure and brought light into the space. "I wanted to address the room structurally in the traditional mission style by breaking up the wall with the wainscoting and adding the designs above the doors. Yet it's not done in a heavy Spanish colonial way," says Kintisch.

"The Spanish colonial revival generally ignored the quality of light within the house," Hedborg notes, "and it seems I always end up doing these Spanish houses with a living room on the dark side, like the Milches'. So we used a warm, light-hued palette and keyed the quality of light in the shadows." His background in painting becomes apparent in his handling of the walls: "It is like a painting; the walls and furniture reflect a warm shadow as opposed to a cold shadow." Throughout, the designers used colors from the garden, especially from the orange tree and a bougainvillea that flowers profusely.

In vernacular Spanish architecture there is a tradition of putting broken tiles at doorways and hearths to ward off evil spirits, and Kintisch chose to express that in the Gaudíesque fireplace made of bits of colored tile. "And because the family is very expressive and artistic," she says, "I wanted to treat the tile as pieces of color, like brushstrokes in a painting."

Where the traditional Spanish house would have tile stair risers in a variety of patterns, the risers of the entrance hall stair are stenciled in geometric patterns that contrast with the bougainvillea design that climbs up the steps. "I wanted it to read like tile but not be imitation tile. It's very important for me to maintain the integrity of a house, but I'm not trying to do things that are historically correct," Kintisch explains.

Inside, the house continues to evolve with the addition of furnishings, decorative elements, and art that Rita collects. Artist Heidi Wianecki and Rita like junkstore finds, but Wianecki also created custom furniture and laid every piece of tile on the patio paving she designed from broken bits of Malibu and terra-cotta tiles.

"The Spanish style encompasses the mundane to the sacred," says Kintisch. "True to the Spanish culture, there is the combination of earthiness and incredible refinement." And Hedborg adds why this style of house remains relevant today: "Spanish houses that are fifty, sixty years old or older are comfortable and livable; they are laid out with courtyards, balconies, rooms to be public in and rooms to be quiet in—elements that make them what I call 'grand bourgeois.'"

Below: The original side courtyard is highlighted by an exedra fountain of tiles thought to be from either the Malibu or Catalina Island potteries.

Right: Worn and weathered Mexican-style benches, pots, and contemporary outdoor furniture complete the outdoor courtyard room.

Above: French doors open the dining room to the side courtyard. The stencilwork is a free interpretation of Spanish patterns typical of the work of immigrants at the time the house was built.

Opposite: A skylight brightens the entrance hall, and the stair risers were painted to imitate geometric tilework. In contrast to the formal curves of the original wrought iron stair rail, the stencil border along the stair wall is a free pattern of bougainvillea.

Opposite: The walls and fabrics of the living room are in autumnal colors cooled by creams and greens.

Right: The living room fireplace was designed as a Gaudí-like work made up of bits of colored tile.

Below: Although large, the truss-ceilinged, missionlike living room is warm, with its texture woven from the wall stenciling, furniture, and fabric colors.

Gordon Kaufmann, *architect*

Edward Huntsman-Trout, *landscape architect*

An overgrown pergola flanks one side of the formal terraced garden and leads from the house to the pool house.

Kamins House

BEVERLY HILLS, 1928–1933

British-born architect Gordon Bernie Kaufmann worked often in the Spanish-Italianate varieties of what he characterized as the "new style" of California houses. Here, an Andalusian facade and Monterey balconies mask the Italianate style of this classical Spanish-style house. Its plain walls, wrought iron details, courts, loggias, balconies, terraces, fountains, and gardens are all part of a unified ensemble of house and landscape on a site backing up to a woody ravine and the lush golf course of the Beverly Hills Country Club.

Kaufmann was educated at the London Polytechnic and the Royal College of Art, but the formal inspiration for his work was the designs of Sir Edwin Lutyens. Kaufmann came to Los Angeles in the early 1910s after spending a few years in Canada, and by the mid-1920s he had enough commissions to open his own office, where he produced such notable works as the Los Angeles Times Building, La Quinta Hotel in Indio, and Scripps College for Women in Claremont.

Philip and Dorothy Kamins bought the house over twenty years ago, but no structural changes have marred the house as completed in 1930. "We had been looking for about a year," Dorothy recounts, "and when we walked in we knew it was right for us." Kaufmann collaborated on this project with landscape architect Edward Huntsman-Trout.

"The rear terraces are magnificent," Dorothy adds. "All the different levels and tiers . . . you can meander and always find a new place to settle." The spacious outdoor rooms step down the lot, past the loggia terrace, drop down to the reflecting pool and farther to the swimming pool terrace, and terminate at a hidden grotto fountain that overlooks the ravine. The whole is a masterpiece of brilliant sunlight and deep shadows. Beyond the garden walls, the jacaranda, bougainvillea, and other hedges of the golf course extend the landscape into the distance.

Inside, Kaufmann carefully scaled the double-height stair hall with its wrought iron balcony that leads up to the broad upstairs hall and the bedrooms. "We were not specifically looking for a Spanish house," comments Dorothy, but "all the other houses we saw had monstrous living rooms, entertainment rooms, and dining rooms. This house was just what we wanted because it was more compact and comfortable." The real living, she says, takes place on the terraces. The original owner, Paul M. Helms of Helms Bakery, even had a bread oven beside the outdoor barbecue.

Plain stucco walls, simple window grills, and a simple volume reflect the stately simplicity that revivalist architects prized and that raised the appreciation for the Andalusian farmhouse style.

Above: A loggia terrace designed to be formal, with a wall separating it from the lower gardens, is for outdoor dining and entertaining.

Opposite: Despite the Andalusian farmhouse references of the front facade, the fountain facing it is formal and classical, with a scalloped double basin. Certain elements, however, are derived from the California vernacular, such as the front wall of Palos Verdes stone and an openwork screen.

The east loggia, an open-air living room adjacent to the dining terrace, is paved in Spanish-style tilework; its shuttered window looks out to the informal gardens.

Above: The reflecting pool is submerged to allow views of the entire garden from the terrace.

Right: A lanai, an entire wing of the house, flanks the reflecting pool. Tiled paths and clipped hedges add to the garden's classical formality.

Ricardo Legorreta, *architect*

Lehrer & Sebastian, *landscape architects*

Elemental and basic are two words often used to describe vernacular works like peasant houses and working ranchos. Yet those words are perfectly applicable to, and complimentary of, the high-style designs of Mexican architect Ricardo Legorreta. The entrance to this house presents a stucco wall of repetitive slit windows that creates mystery and poetry through the contrast of light and dark.

Greenberg House

BRENTWOOD, 1991

Mexico City-based architect Ricardo Legorreta says, "Historically, the Mexican people have built with high walls, ample spaces, color, and textures, and it is from these elements that I designed the Greenberg house. Mystery, surprise, color, and sensual richness—these are the results of their use." He adds, "Most characteristic of my work is the wall, which I use here as a building element and a symbol. It's an abstraction inspired by several indigenous Mexican sources—the *zócalos* and plazas, churches, colonial haciendas, the simplicity of vernacular village architecture. And there are the spatial arrangements of pre-Hispanic ceremonial structures." Legorreta's concrete-and-plaster buildings capture the spirit of adobe within the parameters of modernity.

The Greenberg House reestablishes the essential appeal and appropriateness of the Mexican house for Southern California. Whether stone, mortar, or sundried mud bricks, the Mexican house is the source for Legorreta's gay colors and indoor-outdoor relationships. Regional connections between Mexico and Southern California might be expected, since the high walls that protected haciendas and missions are ever-present in the Southern California landscape. However, California's Spanish revival generally bypassed its regional and Mexican sources for imports from Spain.

In Mexico, a different development occurred, partly instigated by the late artist Jesus ("Chucho") Reyes, a contemporary of Frida Kahlo, who did much to awaken Mexican designers to their own folk culture and turn them away from imported sources, especially the French decorative style that had left a strong imprint since the 1930s.

Legorreta studied architecture in Mexico City, absorbing the lessons of José Villagran and Luis Barragan, the two Mexican modernists with whom he is most often associated. "I learned modernist theory at the university," says Legorreta, "but artist Chucho Reyes helped me to see the beauty and vitality of traditional structures; he taught me the art of seeing with innocence." Since opening his firm in 1963, Legorreta has done much to distance himself from his earlier mentors, and this is recognizable in his large body of work—houses in Mexico and California; Camino Real hotels in Ixtapa, Cancun, and Mexico City; offices for IBM in Mexico City and Roanoke, Texas; and his recent civic work, the Pershing Square plaza in downtown Los Angeles and the master plan and buildings of the National Center of the Arts in Mexico City.

So much of Legorreta's work is famous—or infamous—for the "wild paintbrush" he uses. "I think of color as another building material. With it you can accentuate shapes or you can deny the mass of a building form," Legorreta explains. The colors of Mexico are unlike their Spanish equivalents—the pinks are more brilliant, the purples more sonorous, the yellows more acid, and the greens more tropical.

"When I met Audrey and Arthur Greenberg we talked for hours," says Legorreta; they wanted to replace a Spanish house they had lived in for twenty-five years. "We had become aware of contemporary Mexican architecture in the Barragan tradition," explains Audrey Greenberg, "and it was the sense of high walls, the colors, the high drama and very secluded, mysterious feeling that we wanted for our house. Legorreta really listened to what we were saying.... He came back with a little model of the house. That model, with few exceptions, is basically what we have now."

Unlike a traditional house, the Greenberg House is a spiritual retreat, or secret garden; its plain walls give the appearance of an ancient monument. Eighty-foot palm trees are used as architectural accents against Legorreta's cubic shapes, which are layered and angled, creating an enigmatic sculpture of light. Inside, the house is welcoming, with lofty and sensuous skylighted spaces that encourage movement from place to place. "I think of architecture as sculpture," says Legorreta. "The framing of the view, the massive walls, and the simplicity of materials add harmony and mystery to the space."

"At the rear terrace there are walls, water, and earth colors—three primary elements from the Mexican culture," Legorreta continues. Stepped grass terracing leads down from the rear terrace to the L-shaped pool. A Jacuzzi tower adjacent to the pool has a hot pink trellis that illuminates the area around it when sunlit. The rest of the rolling lawn is punctuated with a few coral trees, yucca plants, and jacarandas brought from the Greenbergs' previous garden.

It is the totality of the architecture and landscape that is the hallmark of Legorreta's design. "The house is modern, colorful, simple, and elegant, but the more I live in it the more I feel it is also a traditional Mexican house," Audrey concludes.

Each room has its own atmosphere and assumes a different character throughout the changing light of day. Color, like the sky-blue interior courtyard off the breakfast room, is used as an eye-catching accent.

Blue sky, gravel, and yellow- and mustard-colored walls are linked in the front facade, where succulents and a stand of palm trees make a desertscape out of the motor court. The front door is hidden from view behind the front wall.

Opposite: Overscaled Mexican pots are on the rear terrace, where a floor-to-ceiling window brings the view into the dining room.

Above: The rear facade is dominated by two angled towers, one for the master bedroom suite and the other for the library, with the living room between them. The angled ramp is an exterior stair leading to a study off the master bedroom.

Above and opposite: The geometric design of the Jacuzzi pavilion, left, is echoed in the swimming pool, and even in the "breezeway" path between the garage and the house.

Above: In the dining room, a deep-set window adds to the adobelike character of the house. The Renaissance-style chairs, square wood tables, tapestry, and crystal chandelier had been a part of the owners' earlier house.

Opposite: Throughout the house, interior designer James P. Sams designed the traditional, almost primitive elements of the walls to meld with contemporary art and antiques, as seen in the entrance hall, where a large painting is accompanied by a Spanish table, candelabra, and a large charger.

Wallace Neff, *architect*

Edward Grensbach, *renovation architect*

Deborah Nevins, *landscape architect*

A circular entrance court was unusual for the twenties, but under architect Wallace Neff's influence it was copied by other architects and builders of the period. Its Spanish source is unclear, but it is certain that Neff derived inspiration from his European travels or his Beaux-Arts education at Massachusetts Institute of Technology. The walls of the court are veneered with local Palos Verdes stone.

Former Niblo House

BEVERLY HILLS, 1926

The Fred Niblo House, a 1926 Spanish-Mediterranean design by Wallace Neff, is most unusual for its circular plan that forms a grand enclosed motor court. It sits atop a Beverly Hills mountain where its unique plan provides views in many directions.

The movie colony had a particular liking for Neff, and throughout his career he designed houses for a number of studio heads and film celebrities. Fred Niblo, who commissioned the house, was a prominent figure in the Hollywood film world of the 1920s. As a director for Metro-Goldwyn-Mayer, he was credited with such popular films as *Ben Hur*, *The Three Musketeers*, *Mark of Zorro*, *Blood and Sand*, *Camille*, *Mysterious Lady*, and *The Enemy*.

The Niblo house was once owned by Jules Stein, the founder of Music Corporation of America (MCA), who added the pool at the rear terrace and a glazed loggia, and who remained in the house for forty years. Katharine Hepburn recalls in her autobiography playing croquet with Spencer Tracy on the lawn when she lived there.

The current owners refurbished the house, restoring it to the glory of the 1920s. Edward ("Ted") Grensbach, the restoration architect, understood the strength of Neff's design and insisted that the house be put on a "pedestal" so it could be better seen. Previously the house was flush with the ground; Grensbach gave it a visual lift by lowering the courtyard eighteen inches.

Inside, Neff had installed freely interpreted classical paneling and moldings that imparted an Old World spirit. The present owners have made only minor structural changes and upgraded the kitchen and the bathrooms. "We modified a couple of little rooms on the upper story where we enclosed the verandas to make proper-sized rooms for our children. But overall we have kept its original boundaries," they say.

When the current owners first saw the house, the front facade was covered with a dark green "cloth" of foot-thick ivy. "Ted Grensbach suggested we take it off, but I was really quite terrified by what it might look like," says the owner. "He said, 'I promise you'll find you have a beautiful stone house under it.'" The owner agreed but, being overly anxious, asked that the work be done while she was away. "When I came back, here was this pale, lovely Palos Verdes-stone house waiting for me. It was quite a transformation."

Architect Wallace Neff tended to simplify and broaden Spanish forms. On the rear loggia he emphasized the horizontality of the arcade, compressing the height of the upper story. His style of Spanish house joined with classical elements of Italian designs led to the unique development of the California Mediterranean idiom.

Above: A former gateway leading from the motor court to the kitchen area has been filled in with custom-designed tiles.

Opposite: When Jules Stein owned the house, he added a classical-style pool to the upper terrace.

Left: The house is entered through a broad white arch, but little other ornament decorates the motor court facade except the bottle-glass and trifoil pediment windows.

Above: The cresting baroque Spanish gate leads from the motor court to the croquet lawn.

Above and opposite: Architect Wallace Neff designed the large rear loggia not merely as an arcaded passageway, but also as a tile-paved outdoor dining room.

Arthur B. and Nina Zwebell, *architects*

Craig Wright, *restoration and interior design*

At the Andalusia Courtyard Apartments the pointed-arch fireplace, tiled quatrefoil fountain, and a wooden balcony are forms derived from the farmhouses and small town and city structures found in Andalusia, Spain.

The Andalusia Courtyard Apartments

HOLLYWOOD, 1926

"The Zwebells brought a sense of authenticity and tremendous individual privacy to the courtyard apartment building," says designer Craig Wright of the originators of the deluxe courtyard apartment building in Los Angeles. Arthur and Nina Zwebell built the Andalusia apartments in 1926, and during that busy decade they established an architectural and interior design firm, contractor's office, and period furniture factory. In 1990, together with his business partners Don and Alice Wilfong, Wright acquired this fine Spanish-revival building.

The Zwebells' source for the courtyard apartment style was the Spanish courtyard house, which had influenced apartment courts from the 1880s on and become extremely popular in the 1920s. During that decade Arthur was contractor and Nina interior designer for their eight courtyard apartment projects, six of which were in the Spanish-revival style.

The Andalusia established their reputation. Arthur modeled it on Andalusian prototypes, so the front facade is fairly plain. A wood-rail balcony runs across the second floor, and a round arch defines the central opening leading to the courtyard. Seen as a singular building with low side wings, the Andalusia virtually hides its interior courtyard; the two front wings are actually garages flanking the motor court.

In the courtyard are wood and wrought iron balconies, windows of different sizes and shapes, and a landscaped garden and tiled fountain. The courtyard is used as a kind of vestibule and creates a private space for the multiple units. Each apartment has a terrace, balcony, or patio that offers another transition from public to private space.

The Zwebells' apartment designs were spatially complex, with double-story living rooms and mezzanines, and were individualized with fireplaces, beamed ceilings, and unique window shapes. The Zwebells had a special corner tower apartment for themselves, and their niece lived there and owned the Andalusia until her death in 1990, renting to such celebrities as Clara Bow, Claire Bloom, Cesar Romero, Marlon Brando, and Louis L'Amour early in their careers.

Wright reflects on how such apartments fulfilled a particular need. "At that point, people were coming out from New York and other cities," he explains. "Among them were hopeful screenwriters or those lucky enough to have a job at Paramount and either two suits or two dresses. They had no possessions and just wanted a furnished apartment." The Andalusia provided the appropriate credenzas, dining tables, chairs, sofas, and chests, which Nina Zwebell designed and Wright reupholstered with Mallorcan fabrics and now offers for his tenants' use.

When Wright and the Wilfongs purchased the Andalusia, they restored it without altering its character. Wright replaced plumbing and wiring and added air-conditioning; he repaired weathered doors and windows and had broken tiles copied or refurbished. Landscape architect Robert Fletcher brought the garden back to its original appearance, and Wright removed a later addition, a swimming pool at the rear of the site.

The prized tower apartment that was once the Zwebells' became Wright's new home. It is the most dramatic apartment in the Andalusia and includes three fireplaces, a double-height living room, a tiled staircase, and two round rooms in the tower. "I'm a collector who is actively experimenting and studying," says Wright. "So my apartment is almost like a laboratory. It is never finished, always in process with piles of books and pictures stacked against the walls."

"When visitors come into the courtyard and into my apartment, they say they're in another world and another time," says Wright "but in fact, you are only two hundred yards from Sunset Boulevard, in the heart of Hollywood."

The picturesque corner tower apartment is part of the typical Spanish courtyard, where paved walkways are defined by parterres lined in hedges.

Above: In the double-height living room, a tiled staircase leads to the mezzanine library. The room is furnished with an eighteenth-century Chinese Export table, a Genoese armchair, and an antique Samarkand carpet.

Left: Beside the fireplace is a pair of eighteenth-century Venetian side chairs.

Opposite: Opening directly to a private patio, the bedroom is another double-height space, with stairs leading to the master bath.

Leonard Hill and Ann Daniel House

Former Willis Mead House

Lester Scherer, *architect*

Thomas Michaeli of M2A, *renovation architect*

Thomas Cox, *landscape architect*

Casa de las Campanas is set in an extraordinary tropical landscape, but its name derives from a triple-story clock-and-bell tower at the rear of the house.

Casa de las Campanas

HANCOCK PARK, 1926–1928

In 1926, Willis Howard Mead, one of the owners of a large lumber company, built a Spanish-revival house that remains one of the most romantic of that era. Accenting the picturesque massing of the facade are robust carvings on the chocolate-brown wood balcony and bay window and intricate detailing on the creamy limestone door surround, both of which betray the Moorish elements in the Spanish design.

Credit to architect Lester Scherer for the design of the house has been largely obscured by claims made by the Meads' daughter, Lucile, who lived in the house until her death in 1986. "[My] original sketch is still the foundation of the present floor plan," she wrote in 1929 in her sorority newsletter. It is unclear whether Lucile actually had real design ability or simply drew a floor plan; but there is no mistaking that she did claim design "ideas." Referring to an unnamed architect, Lucile stated that she had "work[ed] on very thorough plans with a young man only a year older than myself, who was particularly artistic and original, and who had a faculty for working out almost any idea we suggested."

Lucile worked for two years planning the house and supervising its construction, and she took full responsibility for the interior decoration and furnishings. She also collaborated daily with the gardeners, carpenters, woodcarvers, tile setters, masons, and bricklayers. Since her father manufactured tile, Lucile designed some in new colors and patterns for the house. Her best work is in her own apple-green bathroom with its unique, egg-shaped sunken tub.

The front garden, originally landscaped with volcanic rock and a few tall palms and cactus, has been transformed to a lush and exotic planted oasis. Bird of paradise plants flank the entrance, softening the geometries of the square stone surround and the deep-set, rounded-arch door.

Inside, to the left of the entrance hall in a tall octagonal stair hall, is a chandelier made to surround a bronze bell stamped with the name *San Juan* and the date *1790,* thought to have been brought to California by Spanish padres for a small mission church near San Diego. Mead rescued a number of artifacts—a walnut-paneled dining room, a conservancy, and numerous fixtures—from a large Victorian estate demolished in 1924. Their presence in the house accounts for the occasional confusion of styles in this otherwise well-integrated design.

The double-height living room is 23′ by 45′, and at one end, a decorative tiled stairway leads to a mezzanine and Lucile's painting studio. The carved and painted beamed ceiling is exceptional. "Mead had access to rather spectacular materials," explains Leonard Hill, the current owner. "The beams are of hard kiln-dried, twenty-foot-span redwood and Mead was able to bring the craftsmen to the house to carve on site."

Ann Daniel and Leonard Hill, both television and movie producers, purchased the house in 1986 and made some modifications. For the interiors, they explain, "we worked with designer Rich Assenberg to incorporate our somewhat eclectic collection of artwork and to create a house that was more than an interior designer's statement of the period." Len Hill continues, "Purchasing the house accelerated our interest in American art pottery—particularly the California potteries like Gladding McBean, Malibu, Alhambra, and Berkeley Faience, as well as Roseville, Weller, and other well-known American potteries of the first part of the century." The tiles in the pool and in the renovated master bedroom suite were modeled on those at the Adamson House (p. 56) and were handcrafted in Topanga Canyon near the site of the Malibu Potteries.

Now the couple is collecting California paintings from the 1920s and 1930s and Spanish colonial carvings. But, Len Hill adds, "the house is probably the penultimate part of our collection, because we were able to acquire the records, original fixtures, and a lot of the original furniture. We were drawn to it as a rare case where something had remained intact as an example of its era."

A glass-and-lath structure, a Victorian orchid house salvaged in 1924, is attached to one side of the main house at the rear courtyard.

Opposite: On the front of the house, a Moorish hanging lamp is next to the Moorish-style balcony of the guest suite.

Above: The broad, arched limestone portal at the front of the house leads to the garage.

Opposite: The daughter of the original owner of Casa de las Campanas designed the moderne wrought iron stair railing after visiting the famous Paris Exhibition of 1925.

Above: Much of the living room's original furniture, ordered from manufacturers in Chicago, Grand Rapids, and New York, remains in the house. The tiled stairs lead to the original owner's daughter's painting studio.

Left: A cabinet in the breakfast room displays pieces of a pottery collection from the 1920s and 1930s. On top are green Roseville pots and vases in the Vista pattern, with images of palm trees. Inside are pieces by Roseville, Rookwood, Weller, and Van Briggle.

Below: Apple-green bathroom tiles were designed by the original owner's daughter and manufactured at her father's tileworks. To the left of the sunken tub is a tall Roseville vase from the 1920s.

Opposite: The kitchen has new appliances, but the unusual tile walls and ceiling are original.

Left: Window lunettes in the breakfast room are stenciled in patterns reflecting the wrought iron grill doors leading to the dining room. The interior designer also used the stencil and grill patterns for the metalwork base of the glass table.

Above: The leaded glass bay windows in the Oriental parlor are designed in Spanish-Moorish patterns.

Roland Coate, Sr., *architect*

Architect Roland Coate, Sr., turned the house toward the arcaded, four-car garage wing of the motor court and reversed the traditional arrangement of rooms.

Former Fudger House

HANCOCK PARK, 1929

"We were looking for a pure Southern California house," says the owner of this Spanish-revival house designed by Roland Coate, Sr., in 1929. The Monterey colonial, with its wood shutters and a Monterey balcony that stands out against smooth white plaster, is in Hancock Park. This long-established pocket of civility is more like the gracious community of Montecito, near Santa Barbara, than other exclusive neighborhoods of Los Angeles because it is reminiscent of simpler times when neighbors relished friendships, family ties, and family histories.

Roland Coate, Sr., had been in partnership with Reginald Johnson and Gordon Kaufmann and opened his own office in 1925. He specialized in houses for established clients in Hancock Park, Pasadena, and San Marino, and his work was particularly appreciated for its large, airy interiors that opened to the outdoors. As a graduate of Cornell University, trained in its Beaux-Arts approach to design, Coate was especially adept at period revival and specialized in Mediterranean and Monterey colonial styles that he felt were appropriate to Southern California.

In his writings, Coate produced some of the most cogent arguments for use of the Spanish style. In "The Early California House, Blending Colonial and California Forms," he asserted:

> In California, the original borrowing was Spanish. The Mission churches were a simple type of what in Mexico, where materials and workmen were more available, was an expression of the Spanish Plateresque. California houses were as nearly like the houses of Andalusia as the crudity of materials and the dearth of workmen could make them. For it was the Spanish province of Andalusia which sent the first soldiers and adventurers to California. But when California became a member of the Union and officials, settlers and artisans came to the capital, Monterey, they found Spanish style not to their liking and they added to them details of New England Colonial houses.

Coate articulated many of the Monterey elements visible in this house: "Spanish massing, some patios, courts, balconies but [New England-style] double-hung windows, wooden casings, molded trims, entrance doors with side lights and doors of four, six and eight panels."

Mrs. Richard Fudger, a young widow with two children, commissioned Coate to design this house on a beautiful site overlooking the golf course of the Wilshire Country Club. "It's our backyard that we don't have to maintain," says the current owner about the golf course, which creates a parklike setting for the house. "There's a stream that cuts through the golf course and in summer, after-hours, we take the kids out there," she says. "They see crayfish in the stream—which they are convinced are lobsters. These are the elements that allow you the fantasy of having your children grow up someplace idyllic and safe. You feel as though you're in a country oasis yet you consciously know that you're smack in the middle of a serious city."

Reversing the traditional house plan, Coate turned this house to face the landscape of the golf course. Therefore, the front of the house is enclosed: the front garden is shielded by a high wall at the street, and a high wall of hedges and tree ferns hugs the path across the front of the house, past the kitchen and breakfast room. The dining room and children's bedrooms open to the side courtyard, and the living room and master suite have magnificent views of the golf course behind the lot.

"I appreciate the exteriors most, since the house is absolutely surrounded by wildlife," adds the owner, who is a trustee of the Los Angeles Zoo. "The greatest joy for me is looking out this enormous bay window in the master bedroom to an unobstructed view of green in every direction, with hills peeking through the trees. We see owls in the trees and we've seen what I would clearly say are hawks and possibly an eagle."

The owners recognize the abstract beauty underlying the Spanish style, and their strong, spare interiors reflect that appreciation. "There is something about the walls, something about the stability. They seem so massive, like they were there before you were, and they'll be there when you're gone."

A delicate wrought iron balcony opens the master bedroom to the rear garden and a view of the Wilshire Country Club golf course. Howard Hughes bought the house in the 1930s when he was seeing Katharine Hepburn, and they used to go through the back gate to play golf.

The wood shutters and raised main floor, seen from the motor court, reveal architect Coate's appreciation for the Mallorcan forms of the Balearic Islands; he once wrote: "Majorca . . . is Spanish, but . . . its architecture is . . . altogether Majorcene."

Above: The wide ceiling cornice and the broad, double-hung windows in the dining room show the strength of architect Coate's original design.

Opposite: A Spanish colonial revival Monterey balcony runs the length of the street facade, where tree ferns and a hedge add privacy to the house and the path that leads from the driveway to the side kitchen entrance.

Former Parker Toms House

Wallace Neff, *architect*

Essentially a Spanish farmhouse design, this house reflects architect Wallace Neff's flirtation with the adobework and plank shutters of the Southwest and of the local California rancho.

Lamb House

SAN MARINO, 1924

Of all of the communities in Southern California, San Marino and Pasadena have traditionally encouraged period-style architecture. Architect Wallace Neff's career flourished there throughout the 1920s and 1930s through his superb rendering of the Spanish revival style. His 1924 Parker Toms House was particularly admired by the Spanish-style proselytizer and postmodern architect Charles Moore, who was well known for his own exaggerated classical imagery, and who probably appreciated Neff's design for its strong character and its Mexican-Spanish rancho elements. One can easily imagine that Neff, like Moore, thoroughly enjoyed and celebrated his architectural fantasies and did not always take himself or his work too seriously.

Inspiration for the Parker Toms House, now owned by Dr. and Mrs. Richard Lamb, comes from the Southwest, where the adobe wall is paramount. Perhaps to better fit the rancho style to the privacy of a suburban neighborhood, Neff omitted from the front of the house elements typical of the hacienda, such as the open forms of a portal porch and Monterey balcony, reserving them for the rear, more private facade. At the front, a curving driveway sprawls across the lawn, accenting the horizontality of the low living room wing with its repetitive, deep-set windows. Like the California houses built during the Mexican and early American periods, the house has a Monterey tile roof. However, overtones of the Southwest appear in the window shutters of simple wood plank.

"We moved here in January 1977, when we bought the house from writer Joseph Wambaugh," says Mrs. Lamb. "Dee and Joe Wambaugh lived in the house for a long time and raised their children here." Sometime in the 1940s or 1950s, everything on the interior had been painted green, including the beams. "Joe got the original workmen who had built the house to restore it," says Dr. Lamb. "When we bought it, it was restored to the way it had been. We haven't changed very much because we like it the way Dee and Joe did it." The Lambs even bought much of the Wambaughs' modern Mexican ranch-style furniture, including the leather sofas in the living room.

"The tennis court was put in by Joe during the 1970s," says Dr. Lamb. "The city denied Joe a variance to build it so he and his attorney figured out that if you pave over part of your property and happen to pave it in red and green with white stripes, nobody can stop you." Wambaugh put up a removable net and lights on one side of the house and planted trees around the paving. When the city still fought it, he wrote a satirical piece for the *Los Angeles Times* about the stuffiness of the San Marino mayor, city council, and planning commission. "It made fools of them all," Dr. Lamb continues, "and they backed off at that point because they didn't want any more articles. I guess they were kind of glad to end the battle, not only because of the article, but because Joe made the tennis court public; he let it be known that anybody who wanted to play tennis could come over and play."

The tennis court was only briefly visible from the street, since Wambaugh's trees grew quickly. "When we moved in, we'd look out the kitchen window and see total strangers on the court," says Mrs. Lamb. "They'd introduce themselves and say they were playing tennis there like they always did because Joe said it was all right." Gradually the Lambs discouraged this and Neff's inward-turning house has returned to being the private retreat it was designed as.

Below: The simple brackets at the juncture of the two stories are similar to viga posts seen in Southwest pueblo design. A sculptural curved stair leads up to the master suite.

Opposite: The living room wing is a low, horizontal form with a Monterey-style flat tile roof and shuttered post-and-lintel windows.

Opposite, above: The most decorative aspects of the house are the elaborately painted ceilings that reflect Spanish hues and patterns.

Opposite: Forms are simple and ample in the spacious living room, which is accented by rough wood trusses and a Southwest-style corner fireplace, giving the overall impression of a plain, mission-style Mexican rancho.

Above: The straightforward stairhall is decorated only with tile risers, a simple wrought iron rail, and a carved column that appears to be a roughly carved vernacular piece.

Former James Degnan House

Paul Williams, *architect*

At the entrance, a robustly sculpted door surround, a pierced balcony, wall vents, and filigree grillwork all reflect Spanish plateresque influence. Architect Paul Williams designed in a broad range of historicist styles, but he displayed his greatest strength in richly detailed European versions.

Edelbrock House

LA CANADA, 1927

An ornate sixteenth-century doorway in Osuna, Spain, was the key design source for the entrance to this house in La Canada, designed by architect Paul Williams in 1927 for lawyer James Degnan. The typical Spanish plateresque, or "silversmith," style also appears around the ornate doorway in the form of exuberant stucco ornament, tall finials, and a projecting semicircular balcony above. The style can be traced to early-sixteenth-century Italian sculptors and artisans, who were brought to Spain to execute tombs and altars for Spanish nobles and church officials. Such elements as the pilaster paneled with arabesques or the candelabra shaft were applied to buildings by Spanish architects.

Deeply pierced window openings and elaborate wrought iron window grills display Williams's understanding of this unique Spanish interpretation of the classical style. The terraced facades of the ballroom and living room, however, are more typically Italianate, with arched loggias, ornate half-columns, and della Robbia-like glazed terra-cotta panels. Williams also used classical geometry in the cubic volumes of the 25′ by 25′ entrance hall and in the smaller study.

In many ways, the Edelbrock House also displays the baroque forms of eighteenth-century Spanish palaces, in which rooms were finished in plain, sand-finish plaster and left a natural color to dramatize brilliant drapery and upholstery fabrics. The grand style of the house is most apparent in the entrance hall, called both the ballroom and the marble room. It is defined by a black-and-white checkerboard marble floor, a twenty-foot ceiling with wood beams and hand-stenciled panels, and a skylight. Cast-plaster relief panels decorate the upper wall.

In the expansive living room, the open-beamed ceiling is hand painted in colorful, geometric detail. An ornate, cast-concrete fireplace dominates one wall while another has three arched loggia doors. In the dining room, Dr. Edelbrock explains, "the dining table was a Spanish dough table. They would roll the bread dough on top and then place it in the shallow cabinet below to rise before baking."

The Edelbrocks bought the house in 1957. "We moved in when I was five years old," says daughter Christina, "and I remember how I first thought the steam radiators sounded like dragons in the basement." In view of the moody, parklike setting with its tiled and sculpted fountains, lush koi ponds, medieval-style garden furniture, and sylvan grottoes, the house certainly could seem like something out of an era of dragons and young maidens.

Medieval-style garden furniture and reflecting pools bring an unusual, cloisterlike atmosphere to the lush terraced gardens at the rear of the house. On the far right, the loggia is accented above with scalloped oculi.

Above: An octagonal, Spanish-tiled fountain is the focal point of one part of the garden, where a classical balustrade defines the terracing of the landscape.

Right: The niche of the living room terrace is decorated with an Italianate, della Robbia-style glazed terra-cotta plaque depicting the Virgin and Child.

Architect Paul Williams used garden follies typical of eighteenth- and nineteenth-century Europe, here in the form of a rustic tree-limb hut for the Degnan gardens, where the fanciful natural forms suit the rugged La Canada setting.

Above, left: For the breakfast terrace, architect Paul Williams designed an overscaled arcade similar to one used a few years earlier at El Paseo, a Spanish revival-style courtyard structure in Santa Barbara.

Above: The classical restraint of the entrance hall is noted in its proportions—a cubistic 25′ by 25′ space with a twenty-foot ceiling—and in its marble paving, smooth walls accented above with cast plaster reliefs, and the simple open staircase. Some of the Spanish furnishings here came from William Randolph Hearst's San Simeon estate.

Former E.W. "Fannie" Wilkins House

Kirtland Kelsey Cutter, *architect*

The Smith house, poised on the edge of a hill with views over a golf course to the ocean, reflects architect Kirtland K. Cutter's Spanish colonial-revival mode; his designs have the strength and cubistic simplicity of the work of early modernist Irving Gill while incorporating ornate detail.

Smith House

PALOS VERDES ESTATES, 1927

Before Cabrillo explored California in the sixteenth century, a tribe of Native Americans inhabited the peninsula later called Rancho de los Palos Verdes, southwest of Los Angeles. They lived in the hills, and because of their eventual association with the San Gabriel Mission, the tribe was known by the name Gabrielinos. In 1927, architect Kirtland Kelsey Cutter built a hillside house for E.W. (Fannie) Wilkins on the terraced lands that had belonged to the Gabrielinos. Although Spanish in design, in siting it shares a spirit with the indigenous Indian dwellings. For the last thirty years it has housed Annette and Russell Smith's collection of artifacts of the ancient culture and of other primitive peoples.

Cutter, who designed the house as one of a pair (the adjacent house was for Mr. and Mrs. William M. Sutherland), collaborated on the landscape with Frederick Law Olmsted, Jr. When built, each house had a view to the other's garden, but today, trees and shrubbery have obscured that original relationship and the Smiths' front lawn is stone-paved as an entrance courtyard. However, at the rear, little has affected the expansive vistas over the golf course to the ocean. Terra-cotta pots decorate the walls that flank the hillside stairway, and an upper-level balcony, mid-level terrace, and lower-level loggia open the house to its splendid setting.

When Cutter moved from Spokane, Washington, to settle in Southern California, he was in his early sixties. The Palos Verdes community offered him the opportunity to work in the Spanish idiom, and his numerous commissions there earned him a fine reputation.

Designer Paul Frankl leased the house for some time, and after his death, his widow, Mary, sold off much of the furniture, including the plain white dining room table that Annette Smith acquired. "Paul Frankl had carpeted the house and furnished it in the style of the 1930s," says Smith. "I had plenty of Indian and Oriental rugs but I like bare floors, so I took up the carpeting." Carpeting covered the entrance stair, masking beautiful Spanish-tile risers.

The Smiths' collection of artifacts has brought to the house essential colors and forms that resonate with the earthy Spanish architecture. Natural colors, particularly brown, predominate in the ethnic objects that fill the house like displays in a natural history museum. There are also natural woods, fibers, shells, raffia textiles, mineral specimens, and fossils. Annette Smith says, however, "I think this house is white," explaining very matter-of-factly her painterly interpretation of it. "I love color but I'm not one to live with a lot of color. I am a painter and the house is my palette. I love brown, black, and blue, so that's what I've added." Throughout, there are the chocolate-browns of Spanish wooden balconies and beams, the blacks of wrought iron grills, and the rich blues of Spanish tiles, trim, and ceiling stenciling.

The house rises from a lush garden and a Palos Verdes stone-paved courtyard; its deep-set windows and medieval-like overhanging upper story betray architect Cutter's spare Andalusian farmhouse sources.

Opposite: Immediately inside the front door, Spanish-tiled stairs lead to the upstairs bedrooms. On the right, a Mexican "tree-of-life" ceramic adorns a Chinese chest.

Above: The resonant Spanish-blue dining room walls emphasize the curve of the doorway—a shape derived from the structural form of the bracket or attached column that became a motif in California's Spanish moderne work. The long, slender dining table is by modernist designer Paul Frankl, who once leased the house.

Above: A comfortable room on the lower level of the three-story house shows the broad eclecticism of the Smiths' furnishings and artwork—relaxed, unplanned, and personal.

Opposite: Arched doors create a clear passage and a view through the rooms at the front of the house, on either side of the entrance.

Former Donald Lawyer House

John Winford Byers, *architect*

Russell Barto, *renovation architect*

Architect John Byers was a Hispanophile who understood high-style design as well as the rich craftsmanship of vernacular traditions. He designed the Palos Verdes house by mixing Spanish farmhouse and Mexican hacienda traditions, in which the casual courtyard is typically the main entrance to the house.

Puri House

PALOS VERDES ESTATES, 1926

This Palos Verdes house, now the home of Kandee Isam Puri and Tunu Puri, was originally built for Donald Lawyer, sales manager for the organization formed prior to the "home association" that eventually became the city of Palos Verdes Estates. In that community, the house is called the First Family House, or Roessler House, since it was also the home of the town's first mayor, Fred Roessler, who bought it only four years after it was completed and lived in it for nearly half a century, when it was a hub of local civic activities.

Architect John Winford Byers was from Michigan, left the United States briefly to teach languages in Uruguay, then returned to California in 1902 to become part-owner and instructor at the Hitchcock Military Academy in San Rafael. He headed the Romance languages department at Santa Monica High School from 1910 to 1920, when he also became an entrepreneur in building in the local Mexican tradition. He founded the John Byers Mexican Hand Made Tile Company, which soon expanded to the John Byers Organization for Design and Building of Latin Houses. After he got his architect's license in 1926—the year he built the Palos Verdes house—he discontinued the construction business to focus on design, working with his assistant and later partner, Edla Muir. His long career lasted into the late 1950s and Byers and Muir designed numerous Spanish-style houses for clients such as Irving Thalberg and Norma Shearer, Buster Crabbe, and J. Paul Getty.

"There was the framework of the existing Byers design, but it needed to be updated to make it function better and to take advantage of the views," says Palos Verdes architect Russell Barto, who remodeled the house for the Puris when they bought it several years ago. The secluded site overlooking the Pacific is surrounded by tropical trees, lush foliage, rolling lawns, and stone footpaths. The property is entered through wrought iron gates leading to an entrance courtyard that Byers had originally designed as an enclosed garden with a pond, in keeping with the concept of a simple Spanish farmhouse. However, Barto and landscape architect Robert Winship made it more formal and plazalike with pebble paving and a three-tiered, nineteenth-century-style fountain copied from one in Guadalajara, Mexico.

The handmade structural and decorative tiles, wrought iron window grills, and stair railing were all designed by Byers. He and his company also produced the cabinetry, light fixtures, bronze hinges, and doorknobs. The stately formal rooms of the entrance hall, living room, and dining room––ideal for the lavish entertaining and official functions of the former mayor—have not been changed.

Barto made one entirely new addition, the pool house, an airy space with a front wall of French doors. A stone-paved rear terrace ties it to the 1926 house and extends to footpaths that lead down the hillside.

Above: At the top of a Palos Verdes hill, the house faces a spacious croquet lawn and has a view of the ocean. In the recent renovation, to take further advantage of the views and to bring more light inside, several upper windows were changed to French-door balconies, copying those originally part of the house; and the solarium's original folding doors that open to the rear terrace were restored.

Right: A guest wing at the entrance courtyard is set back from a wood frame porch that shelters an East Indian carved wood angel.

Architect John Byers's construction company, the John Byers Organization for Design and Building of Latin Houses, did much to promote the skills and crafts of the local Mexicans he employed, and their wrought iron work, tiles, and hardware adorn his designs.

Left: A spiral-form bronze door handle at the main entrance.

Below: Peacocks typical of the Spanish-Moorish style are depicted in the tile fountain in the courtyard.

Opposite: A birds-in-a-cage wrought iron lamp lights the way to the guest suite.

Gavin and Ninetta Herbert House

Former Hamilton Cotton House

Carl Lindbom, *architect*

Diane Johnson, *renovation architect*

Lew Whitney of Rogers Gardens, *landscape architect*

Casa Pacifica, originally intended as a horseman's rancho, is actually a compound of several buildings. The main house, copied from a house in San Sebastian, Spain, is entered through arched doors and a vaulted passageway leading to the enclosed courtyard.

Casa Pacifica

SAN CLEMENTE, 1927

Casa Pacifica, Richard Nixon's former home, was the site of the signing of the SALT II Treaty on June 18, 1979, and was visited during Nixon's presidency by numerous heads of state, diplomats, and other distinguished guests. Ironically, the San Clemente residence had political ties from its inception, since it was built in 1927 by Hamilton ("Ham") Cotton, who was a close friend of Franklin D. Roosevelt and at one time the leader of California's Democratic Party.

As one of the founders of San Clemente, Cotton helped developer Ole Hanson achieve his dream to build a "Spanish village by the sea." Hanson wanted to pattern the development after Mediterranean villages: "I envision a place where the architecture will be all of one type," he wrote in the early 1920s, adding, "I can see hundreds of white walled homes bonneted with red tile, with trees, shrubs, hedges of hibiscus, palms and geraniums lining the drives, and a profusion of flowers framing the patios and gardens. I can see gay sidewalks of red Spanish tile and streets curving picturesquely over the land." Cotton and Hanson provided the city with necessary infrastructure, public buildings, and winding streets that remain in this growing community today, where official architectural guidelines have established the Spanish style for public and commercial buildings.

Although not built as a developer's model home, Casa Pacifica nonetheless became the model used to entice new residents to the town by displaying the most beautiful of Spanish styles. Architect Carl Lindbom, a Scandinavian immigrant who had a thriving historical revival practice in Los Angeles in the 1920s, based his design on a country house in San Sebastian, Spain.

Cotton's vision was appropriate to the San Clemente area and its rich tradition of Spanish history. The community was established by horsemen-rancheros who traded cattle and horses and who had displaced the Spanish padres when the Spanish era drew to a close. By 1845, even the nearby mission of San Juan Capistrano had been auctioned. American ranchers bought up the land, and the railroad and El Camino Real brought tourist trade as well as investors like Hanson and Cotton.

"Roosevelt used to come here by train," says Gavin Herbert, who now owns the house. "The train would stop below the cliff, and he'd be brought up the stairs to the gazebo overlooking the ocean where he and Cotton had some hot poker games."

A thick white wall links the main house to most of the service buildings in what is roughly a circular compound. From the broad, gravel-paved entry court the main house is reached through a tiled, vaulted passage leading to an inner courtyard. Here, on three sides of an outdoor living room, white pillars and wood-beamed ceilings uphold broad portals. Very little has been changed from the original courtyard, although Cotton was responsible for some art deco additions, like the Portuguese tile murals of romantic

Spanish images and the portal floors produced by the tile company that Cotton started during the 1930s.

Nixon bought the house in 1969, cleaned it up (later Cotton family members had let it deteriorate), added a pool and upper terrace where a tennis court had been, and put in palapa-roofed Secret Service stations and bulletproof glass around the pool. Nixon sold Casa Pacifica to the Herberts in 1980; they opened up some windows as French doors for interior light and restored the interiors in the Spanish colonial revival style. "It was my intent to retain the spirit and simplicity of the main house and, by opening the dining room, the kitchen, and master bedroom to the central inner courtyard, the truly Spanish sense of privacy and enclosure was emphasized," architect Diane Johnson says.

Johnson also added pairs of doors to the master bedroom on the ocean side and a small sitting room off the dining room. "Originally, there were only a few little high windows and you didn't have a sense of what was out there," she says. The French doors now provide access to the ocean and the gardens without compromising the house's character.

Architect Lindbom's original rose garden became Pat Nixon's favorite, but a magnolia tree anchors it to an even older political era. "It was a seedling of a magnolia Andrew Jackson had planted at the White House," says Ninetta Herbert, "and Mrs. Nixon brought it here in establishing this as the 'Western White House.'"

A corner courtyard stairway leads to the study, designed as a home office for the house's original owner and later used for the same purpose by President Nixon and by the current owner.

Above: A pair of overscaled stucco posts with step-shaped crowns derived from the Spanish-Moorish style leads from the main house to the pool. The posts were installed recently when the pool-house pavilion/guest suite was added.

Opposite: Tilelike paving in the corridor surrounding the courtyard, added in the 1930s, is based on Spanish and Mexican motifs. The large piers holding the roof are based on northern Spanish courtyard houses.

Above: Thick adobelike walls create deep passageways throughout the house, as from the library to the dining room, shown here.

Opposite: The entrance hall is flanked by deep archways that lead from a small room with leather-and-brass-studded walls to the living room. The floor stenciling, like the leather walls, is derived from Spanish period sources researched by interior designer Claire Robinson.

The wide range of period styles of the dining room furnishings is offset by the low-trussed ceiling, deep-set windows, shutters, and tile floor of the original elegant farmhouse.

Above: The stepped fountain, with a wide-ledge basin for sitting, dominates the courtyard. At the far end is an outdoor fireplace; to its left, a Spanish-style bell tower was deemed a suitable image for the mission-settled location.

Opposite: A patchwork-quilt effect is created by the pattern of brilliantly colored tiles on the fountain.

Acknowledgments

Melba Levick and Elizabeth McMillian wish to thank the residents who graciously allowed us to include their houses in this book, as well as the architects, designers, and organization and foundation heads who generously lent their time for the successful execution of this project: Leslie Heumann, Jean Goodrich, Laura Bridley, Casa del Herrero Foundation, MacElhenny Group, Casablanca Beach Estates, Roger and Christina Battistone; Henry Lenny and Jeffrey Gorrell, Sharpe, Mahan and Lenny; James Lasseter, Margie and Lawrence Schneider, Cleo Baldon, Ann Payne, Malibu Lagoon Museum, David Anawalt; Robert "Buzz" Yudell, Moore Ruble Yudell; Paul and Leah Culberg, Doug and Regula Campbell, Carl Day, Thomas and Claire Callaway, James Chuda, Peter and Nina Anderson, Maryanne Jordan, Kirsten Combs, Greg Fischer, Rita Stern and David Milch, Jarrett Hedborg, Nancy Kintisch, Heidi Wianecki, Barbara Schnitzer, Philip and Dorothy Kamins, Arthur and Audrey Greenberg, Ricardo Legorreta, James Sams, Lehrer & Sebastian, Anna and Rupert Murdoch, Edward Grensbach, Tim Street-Porter, Craig Wright, Alice and Don Wilfong, Leonard Hill and Ann Daniel; Thomas Michaeli, M2A; Thomas Cox, Richard Assenberg, Robert and Amy Bookman, Mrs. Lawrence Robertson, François Henriod, Dr. and Mrs. Richard Lamb, Karen Hudson, Dr. Harold Edelbrock, Christina Montero, Annette and Russell Smith, Candy Isam Puri and Tunu Puri, Russell Barto, Robert Winship, James Barnes, San Clemente City Planning Department, Gavin and Ninetta Herbert, Diane Johnson, Claire Robinson, Lew Whitney, and Rogers Gardens; and a special thanks to Steve Harby, John Chase, Carol MacMurtry, Richard Landry, Diane Kessler, Robert Easton, Tom Schnabel, and Robert Ramirez. We also acknowledge Malibu Ceramic Works whose tile installations grace the Battistone House.